BEYOND PHYSICAL ROMANCE - THE ESSENTIAL FOUR FOR ANY RELATIONSHIP SUCCESS

A PRACTICAL GUIDE TO BUILDING LASTING RELATIONSHIPS WITH THE H-T-R-O FORMULA

KAUSIK ASUTOSH DATTA

Clever Fox® PUBLISHING

Chennai • Bangalore

CLEVER FOX PUBLISHING
Chennai, India

Published by CLEVER FOX PUBLISHING 2025

ISBN: 978-93-6707-932-4

This third book of mine is dedicated to Almighty God and to my beloved father, Asutosh Datta, who has been my pillar of strength through life's trials. Where I stand today is a reflection of his unwavering support and effort. Thank you, my dearest Dad — you are my hero, and you will always remain so.

To my late mother, whose silent sacrifices and unconditional love taught me the essence of a true connection.

And to my family and beloved friends, colleagues, and well-wishers who stood by me through every storm of my life, reminding me what family and friends mean.

CONTENTS

About the Author .... *vii*

About the Book .... *ix*

Introduction .... *xi*

Preface .... *xiii*

Chapter One: Relationship and Good Living 1

Chapter Two: The Foundations of a Lasting Relationship 21

Chapter Three: Building trust through Relationships 32

Chapter Four: Importance of Respect and Boundaries 43

Chapter Five: Friendship and Relationship 57

Chapter Six: Open Communication 70

Chapter Seven: Conclusion 91

ABOUT THE AUTHOR

Er. Kausik P. Datta is an exceptional Global Trainer, Relationship Mentor, and Author with over two decades of experience spanning the automotive industry, health, and personal development. Having collaborated with over a dozen world-renowned automotive brands across more than 12 countries, he has inspired countless professionals and individuals, leaving a lasting impact on both their professional and personal lives.

Passionate about empowering people beyond technical expertise, Er. Kausik P Datta has devoted recent years to exploring the deeper dimensions of human relationships. His own life's journey—including navigating a painful divorce—became the driving force behind this self-help book, aimed at guiding readers towards more meaningful and lasting connections in a digital age where emotional bonds are often overlooked and underestimated.

He is also the founder of The Auto Mentors Hub, a multi-domain initiative that bridges automotive expertise with emotional intelligence, health, and holistic well-being.

Beyond Physical Romance is his third book, following *Life-Changing 46 Guru Mantras from 46 Years* and *The Magical Wand: The Best Version of Yourself*, both available on Amazon.in & Flipkart Platform. His writing is grounded, deeply personal, and profoundly practical — offering tools that heal anyone from the inside out.

With this latest work, Kausik embarks on a heartfelt mission—to ignite conscious, value-based relationships in today's fast-paced modern society and world.

He currently resides in the Middle East and continues to travel, train, write, and guide people toward living richer, more connected lives — emotionally, mentally, and spiritually.

ABOUT THE BOOK

Researchers say that in the present time, the Earth is spinning faster than the twenty-hour daily rotation, and in this fast-paced world, relationships begin with a lot of excitement, but soon the spark dies down, like a deadly weight, it pulls us down.

And why does this happen?

Because we expect more than what is necessary or needed.

Success is not long-lasting, and every relationship in the modern day starts with an attraction which ends up soon. The spark of fire is soon gone.

Life experiences make us strong, and determined and the author, during his sad, weary, and disappointed days of his own life, experiencing the good, bad and ugly, made him create a strong formula based on four important elements called H-T-R-O, which means:

H For Honesty

T For Trust

R For Respect &

O For Open Communication

Each chapter has brief outlines of stories and self-assessment tasks, which will help you to reflect and rebuild any relationship that comes across in your life.

Whether you are single, married, divorced, or awaiting for one, healing from a heartbreak, or all frustrated and lost, this book will serve as an excellent guide and mirror to gain confidence and rebuild your life.

The language used by the author is clear and simple and is suitable for growing and adult age groups. It also acts as a self-help and self-development book and will be out for the public on the author's 51st birthday.

INTRODUCTION

To My Dearest Brother, Kausik

From the very first Raksha Bandhan, you've been more than just a brother by promise—you've been a source of strength, inspiration, and quiet encouragement.

Our bond, which began in the heart of Ethiopia, holds a treasured place in my life. I still cherish the moments we spent together—celebrating birthdays, sharing laughter, and witnessing milestones like the launch of your second book. Those simple, joy-filled gatherings remain etched in my heart as symbols of genuine connection and warmth.

Watching your journey as a writer has been truly inspiring. Each book you've written is not only a reflection of your thoughts but also a window into your heart and the clarity of your vision.

Now, as your third book prepares to greet the world, I couldn't be prouder. This milestone is more than a celebration of your talent—it is a testament to your consistency, your quiet courage, and your unwavering devotion to your craft. With every word you write, your voice grows stronger, more meaningful, and more impactful.

As your sister, it fills me with immense joy to walk beside you—not just on Raksha Bandhan, but through every chapter of your journey. May this book reach hearts far and wide, and may your stories continue to shine light where it's most needed.

With Admiration and Blessings,

Pushpalatha

Aug-2025

PREFACE

Before You Begin — A Heartfelt Invitation

Before you turn the first page of this book, I invite you to pause — truly pause — and look inward. Not just at your partner, not just at your current "relationship status," but at the living, breathing connection you share.

Ask yourself, with courage and compassion:
How strong is your H–T–R–O?

H–T–R–O is not a fancy theory. It is the quiet architecture that holds every healthy relationship upright:

- **H** — Honesty
- **T** — Trust
- **R** — Respect
- **O** — Open Communication

These are not decorative add-ons to love; they are its structural beams. Without them, even the most passionate love can collapse under life's weight.

So, before we go further, I invite you to take a private, no-judgment self-check. This isn't about shaming or blaming — it's about awareness.

1. **Honesty (H)**
   - Do you freely and comfortably share your true thoughts and feelings with your partner — the messy, imperfect, real ones?
   - Does your partner ever keep important truths from you?
   - Are you both transparent about personal and professional matters, even the uncomfortable ones?

2. **Trust (T)**
   - Do you ever doubt your partner's loyalty when they're not around?
   - Have you felt the urge to "check up" on them?
   - Deep down, are you confident they always have your best interests at heart?

3. **Respect (R)**
   - Do you feel valued for who you truly are — not just for what you give or do?
   - In moments of disagreement, does your partner still treat you with kindness and dignity?
   - Can you stand in your individuality without fearing that their love will fade?

4. **Open Communication (O)**
   - How often do you openly talk about feelings, plans, or concerns — not just the logistics of daily life?
   - When you speak, do you feel genuinely heard, not just "listened to"?

- Are you able to address issues as they come up, or do problems quietly stack in the corner, untouched?

Scoring Yourself:

- For every "Yes," give yourself 1 point.
- 10–12 points: Your pillars are solid — keep nurturing them.
- 7–9 points: There are cracks that deserve your attention before they widen.
- 6 or below: The foundation may already be fragile — but awareness is your first step toward repair.

A Moment of Truth — My Story

I didn't always know the value of these four pillars. For years, I believed love alone could survive anything. I thought if two people "truly loved each other," the rest would take care of itself.

I was totally wrong.

I still remember one quiet evening in Nigeria, sitting across from my spouse at the dinner table. We weren't fighting. We weren't even upset. But the silence was heavy — not peaceful, not comfortable. Just… empty.

We had run out of things to say.

It didn't happen overnight. It was the result of years of unspoken hurt, of sidestepping difficult conversations, of letting small cracks go unpatched. Our love hadn't been shattered by betrayal or explosive arguments — it had been slowly starved.

We still loved each other, but without honesty, trust, respect, and open communication, that love couldn't carry the weight of our lives. In the end, it wasn't the absence of love that ended my marriage — it was the absence of the pillars that kept love alive.

Why I Wrote This Book

I can't rewrite my past, but I can offer you a compass for your present and future.

The H–T–R–O formula isn't just a theory I dreamed up in a coffee shop. It's the distillation of lived experience — mine, and the countless stories I've heard from others whose relationships either flourished or faded based on these four pillars.

Whether you want to:

- Heal a strained relationship
- Protect and strengthen a healthy one
- Or simply understand yourself and your partner better

… this book will meet you where you are.

It isn't just a guide; it's a mirror. It may comfort you in some moments and challenge you in others. It will ask you to dig deeper — to move beyond surface-level romance into the grounded, everyday work of building a love that lasts.

We're about to walk together into the heart of what makes connection real, sustainable, and deeply fulfilling. And if you let it, this journey might just change the way you love — forever.

CHAPTER ONE

Relationship and Good Living

What is a Relationship?

This 12-letter word is very funny, cruel, encouraging, and sometimes totally discouraging. A relationship is the cornerstone of a fulfilling life — a source of emotional support, connection, and a profound sense of belonging. Whether with family, friends, colleagues, or romantic partners, meaningful relationships help us weather storms, celebrate joys, and grow into our truest selves. They teach us empathy, trust, communication, and resilience — qualities that hold both personal peace and social harmony together.

Source: iStock

In a world that often feels fast-paced and isolating, strong relationships act like anchors. They remind us we are not walking alone, but are held and lifted by the hearts we choose to journey alongside.

I learned this truth not in a classroom, but during the slow, golden summers I spent in my grandparents' village in Tripura, India — a place where time seemed to have its own gentle heartbeat.

The village sat like a jewel between rolling green hills, with a silver ribbon of river curling around its edges. Mornings began with the sound of roosters greeting the day and the distant toll of a temple bell, its echo melting into birdsong. The dusty paths were lined with neem and tamarind trees, their shadows offering cool refuge from the rising sun.

Afternoons were unhurried. Women drew water from the well while chatting in warm, rhythmic voices. Children chased each other through narrow lanes, their laughter mingling with the faint scent of woodsmoke from kitchens where flatbreads puffed on clay stoves. In the evenings, the air turned softer, carrying the fragrance of jasmine and the sound of crickets in the fields.

It was under such a sky — deep and wide, dusted with starlight — that my grandmother once told me the story of Ravi and Sita.

Ravi was an old man who lived in a modest clay-walled house on the edge of the village. His roof sagged in places, but his small garden bloomed faithfully every season — hibiscus, Tulsi, and marigolds growing in a cheerful rebellion against time.

Every evening, without fail, Ravi would walk slowly to the central square. There, under the shelter of the great banyan tree, he would sit on a worn wooden bench. He never fidgeted. He didn't scan the crowd. He simply sat, watching the sun sink behind the hills, his eyes holding the kind of light that comes from a life well-lived.

People greeted him with polite nods. Children raced past in games of tag. A few elders stopped for short conversations about the weather or crops, but no one lingered long. No one except Meera.

Meera was ten years old, with eyes like two small lanterns — bright, restless, and unafraid to ask questions others avoided. One evening, she wandered up to the banyan and sat beside Ravi, her legs swinging above the ground.

"Uncle," she began, "why do you come here every day?"

Ravi smiled, a slow, gentle curve of the lips that seemed to hold both mischief and melancholy.

"Because," he said, "this is where I found my life's greatest treasure."

Meera tilted her head. "Treasure? Like gold?"

He chuckled softly. "Better than gold. Come back tomorrow, and I'll tell you."

The next evening, Meera returned, still in her school uniform, satchel slung over her shoulder. And so began a ritual.

Over the next weeks, Ravi told her the story in small pieces, never rushing, as though he wanted her to feel the truth, not just hear it.

Years ago, when Ravi was a young man, the village's annual fair was in full bloom. The air was alive with the scent of marigolds, roasted peanuts, and fried pakoras. Stalls overflowed with trinkets, clay toys, and glass bangles that caught the light like shards of rainbow. Musicians played under the banyan, the rhythmic beat of the Dhol mingling with bursts of laughter.

It was there, under the banyan's sweeping branches, that Ravi first saw Sita. She was at a stall buying jasmine flowers, her braid brushing against her back, her smile quick and bright as the morning sun. They exchanged only a few words — nothing remarkable to an onlooker, but to them, it was the opening note of a lifelong melody.

They married the next year. Life was simple but not without its trials. There were seasons when the crops failed, times when illness swept through the village, and years when money was scarce. Yet through it all, they shared the load. They drank their morning tea together under the banyan, spoke in glances during busy market days, and laughed at the small absurdities that life inevitably provided.

Sita had a way of making even the most ordinary days feel like celebrations. She sang while cooking, hummed lullabies to the plants in their garden, and always saved the last piece of mango for Ravi. He, in turn, built her a small swing in the courtyard, repaired it whenever it squeaked, and made sure her jasmine never ran out.

When Sita fell ill, Ravi cared for her with the same quiet devotion he had shown all his life. And when she passed away, the world felt muted, as though someone had drawn a curtain over the sun. But Ravi did not close himself off. Instead, he returned each evening to the banyan tree — not to drown in grief, but to sit in the place where it had all begun, where her laughter still seemed to dance in the air.

One afternoon, Meera came to him with a small gift she had made at school. It was a wooden plaque, the letters uneven but carved with care. The next evening, she fastened it to the bench. It read:

"A place where love lived — and still does."

Ravi ran his fingers over the words, his eyes shining. "Thank you, child," he said. "Now, even when I'm gone, people will know."

Meera eventually left for the city. Life pulled her into its whirl — studies, work, friendships, new beginnings. Yet the memory of the banyan tree stayed with her.

Years later, she returned to the village. The bench was still there, weathered but steadfast. The plaque had faded, but its message was still readable. Sitting there, she realized that love like Ravi and Sita's never truly belongs to only two people. It becomes part of the village's memory, part of its soil, part of every young heart that learns by example what it means to love without conditions.

That is the power of a relationship. It does not end with presence. It lingers in memory, breathes through legacy, and lives on in the quiet, sacred spaces where two hearts once met — and never stopped speaking.

Ravi and Sita's story is not a fairy tale. It did not glitter with riches, nor was it free from hardship. What made it extraordinary was not perfection, but the steady, deliberate way they lived their love.

When we look closely, their life together quietly reflects the four pillars that make any relationship truly lasting:

1. Honesty — Both shared their burdens and their joys openly, never hiding their struggles behind pride or fear. Even silence between them was honest — a silence of comfort, not avoidance.
2. Trust — Sita knew Ravi would keep the promises he made, and Ravi knew Sita's loyalty was unwavering. Trust was not a one-time gift; it was renewed daily through small acts of dependability.

3. Respect — Both valued each other's opinions, even when they differed. Respect was woven into the way they spoke, listened, and made decisions together.
4. Open Communication — Both didn't wait for misunderstandings to grow into walls. They talked through disagreements and shared their dreams, ensuring they moved through life in harmony rather than in parallel isolation.

The banyan bench became a living symbol of these principles — a place where love was planted, nurtured, and remembered. It teaches us that relationships are not measured by grand gestures alone, but by the quiet consistency of showing up for each other, day after day, year after year.

And perhaps the most profound lesson of all is this: love, when rooted in honesty, trust, respect, and open communication, does not end with death or distance. It becomes part of the living world, shaping others long after the people who created it are gone.

There are many different kinds of relationships—from familial and romantic to friendships and casual connections. Broadly, they can be categorized into family relationships, friendships, romantic relationships, and acquaintanceships. Within these, we find further subtypes such as platonic, casual, or open relationships.

Understanding these categories can help individuals navigate their interactions and build healthy, supportive connections. But there's another, less obvious factor that deeply influences every relationship—not the type of relationship itself, but the inner qualities we bring into it.

While healthy relationships thrive on trust, empathy, and respect, they can be quietly damaged by negative emotions and impulses. Ancient Hindu philosophy offers a timeless lens to understand these inner obstacles: the concept of Arisha Varga.

Arisha Varga — The Six Inner Enemies

In Hindu philosophy, **Arisha Vargas** (also called *Shadripu*, "six enemies") refer to six negative emotions or passions that hinder both spiritual and personal growth. These are seen as the primary barriers on the path to **moksha** (liberation) and to harmony in human connections.

They are:

1. **Kama** (Desire/Lust): Excessive attachment to sensual pleasures or possessions.
2. **Krodha** (Anger): Intense negative emotion triggered by frustration or unmet desires.
3. **Lobha** (Greed): Excessive desire for material possessions or wealth.
4. **Mada** (Ego/Pride): Inflated self-importance and arrogance.
5. **Moha** (Attachment/Delusion): Unhealthy emotional attachment that distorts reality.
6. **Matsarya** (Jealousy): Resentment towards others' success, possessions, or happiness.

These are not enemies outside us; they live within us. In relationships, they show up subtly: in a jealous glance, a controlling decision, a prideful refusal to listen. Over time, they can erode trust, warmth, and mutual respect, leaving the relationship brittle.

Let's look at each one, not just as a philosophical idea, but through short stories showing how they play out in real life.

1. Kama — Desire

In relationships, desire can be both a spark and a snare. It drives attraction and ambition, but when it turns into comparison or obsession, it creates dissatisfaction and distance.

Story: Ravi was a successful man with a loving family. But he became obsessed with buying a luxurious car to keep up with his friends. He took loans, worked overtime, and spent less time with his family. Finally, he bought the car—but by then, his health had declined, and his relationships were strained.

Lesson: Desire, when uncontrolled, leads to imbalance. True joy comes from appreciating what you already have.

2. Krodha — Anger

Anger is like fire—it can warm when controlled, but destroy when unleashed. In relationships, uncontrolled anger leaves scars that words can't erase.

Story: Meena, a teacher, lost her temper during class when a student accidentally spilled water on her table. She shouted harshly and punished the child. Later, she learned the student was nervous because of problems at home. Filled with guilt, she apologized, but the damage was done.

Lesson: Anger clouds understanding. In moments of rage, we often wound those we care about most.

3. Lobha — Greed

Greed isn't only about money—it's the hunger to always take more than we give. In relationships, it shows up as possessiveness, selfishness, and imbalance.

Story: A farmer had a goose that laid a golden egg every day. He grew impatient and wanted all the gold at once. He killed the goose, only to find it was just an ordinary bird inside.

Lesson: Greed blinds wisdom. In wanting more, we often lose what we already have.

4. Moha — Attachment / Delusion

Healthy attachment is love; unhealthy attachment is control. When we cling too tightly, we suffocate the very bond we want to preserve.

Story: Radha loved her son deeply, but couldn't accept that he had grown up. She controlled his choices, friends, and career. Eventually, he moved far away to find freedom, leaving her lonely and bitter.

Lesson: Love should be liberated, not imprisoned. Excessive attachment distorts love into control.

5. Mada — Pride / Ego

Ego in relationships builds walls where bridges are needed. Pride resists apology, refuses advice, and demands superiority.

Story: Vikram was a brilliant scholar. Over time, he began to look down on others and rejected advice. One day, during a public debate, a humble speaker exposed his flaws respectfully. Vikram's ego was shattered, and he realized he had stopped learning.

Lesson: Pride closes the heart to growth. Humility keeps relationships alive.

6. Matsarya — Jealousy

Jealousy poisons relationships by turning admiration into resentment.

Story: Neha and Anjali were best friends. When Anjali won a poetry competition, Neha felt jealous instead of happy. She began gossiping and distancing herself. Later, she realized she had let envy ruin a valuable friendship.

Lesson: True friendship celebrates the other's victory as if it were your own.

Recognizing these six enemies is only the first step. Here are practical ways to weaken their grip:

- **Kama (Desire):** Keep a gratitude journal; focus daily on three things you already have.
- **Krodha (Anger):** Practice the "pause"—count to 10 before reacting.
- **Lobha (Greed):** Share your resources—time, attention, or possessions—without expecting return.
- **Moha (Attachment):** Encourage loved ones' independence, even if it feels uncomfortable.

- **Mada (Pride):** Invite feedback and receive it without defensiveness.
- **Matsarya (Jealousy):** Actively praise others for their successes.

Relationships flourish when nurtured by patience, empathy, humility, and generosity. The Arisha Vargas reminds us that the greatest obstacles to connection are often not "out there" but within us. By cultivating self-awareness and practicing mindful responses, we can disarm these inner enemies—and in doing so, build relationships that are deep, joyful, and resilient.

The Six Inner Enemies in Relationships — Impact & Remedies

Arisha Varga	Meaning	Impact on Relationships	Remedy / Practice
Kama	Desire / Lust	Creates dissatisfaction, comparison, and neglect of present bonds	Keep a gratitude journal; focus on what you already have
Krodha	Anger	Damages trust through harsh words and impulsive actions	Pause before responding; practice deep breathing

Arisha Varga	Meaning	Impact on Relationships	Remedy / Practice
Lobha	Greed	Leads to imbalance, selfishness, and resource hoarding	Share time, attention, and resources generously
Moha	Attachment / Delusion	Turns love into control; suffocates independence	Encourage autonomy; respect personal choices
Mada	Pride / Ego	Blocks communication and learning; prevents apology	Seek feedback; embrace humility

Now going onto health:

Every day, thousands silently wage war against an invisible enemy — cancer.

It is not fought on loud battlefields, but in quiet hospital rooms, in sleepless nights, in the private recesses of the soul. Cancer does not just ravage the body; it shakes the spirit.

You can sense it in the faint smell of antiseptic, the cold touch of hospital sheets, and the steady beep of machines that measure every breath. You see it in faces — the hollowed cheeks, the smiles that try to be brave. And you feel isolation when friends' visits grow less frequent, when conversation turns awkward.

> *"Cancer is not just a disease of the body — it is a storm of the soul."*

In our times, cancer knocks on more doors than ever. The reasons may be many — processed diets, relentless stress, environmental toxins, and sleepless nights.

The disease's final stages are brutally painful — not only because of tumors pressing on nerves, but because of the treatments themselves. Radiation burns skin. Chemotherapy steals hair, appetite, and energy. Bank accounts are drained. Spirits, too.

And yet, within each of us lies a quiet flame — a fierce will to live. It may flicker, it may hide under fear, but it is there.

She was twenty when I met her — vibrant, full of dreams, eyes that sparkled with joy.

Then came the diagnosis: liver cancer. She endured, fought, and won that round. Life returned.

Fifteen years later, lung cancer struck. This battle was heavier. Chemotherapy left her weak, nauseous, and drifting into depression. Her eyes dimmed. Even her doctors could not explain the depth of her exhaustion. One day, she whispered, *"I don't want to live like this anymore."*

When I visited, she sat by the window, silent. Remembering her love for pineapples, I began slicing one. The knife slid through golden flesh. The sweet scent filled the room.

She turned her head. Her eyes lit up. And then — a smile. Not polite, not forced — but real.

It wasn't about the pineapple itself. It was about remembering.
Remembering sweetness.
Remembering the feeling of wanting to live.

> *"Sometimes, the will to live begins with something as small as the smell of a pineapple."*

From that day, she began noticing small joys: the warmth of sunlight, the sound of music, the laughter of children. At first, she simply went through the motions. But slowly, those motions became rituals, and rituals became lifelines.

She planted flowers in her rooftop garden. She read books. She cooked not for survival, but for pleasure. She stopped looking inward for sadness and started looking outward for reasons to smile.

Her health stabilized. The scans still showed cancer, but her spirit told a different story.

Today, she is not cured. Pain still comes. Fatigue still visits. But she is *deeply, beautifully alive.* She calls herself a *"patient"* — one who waits with faith, embraces peace in uncertainty, and refuses to let illness steal every corner of joy.

You don't need a grand reason to live — sometimes you just need a small, sweet one:

- The smell of a favorite flower.

- A song that makes you sway.
- The feel of soil between your fingers.
- The warmth of sunlight through a window.
- A fruit you loved as a child.

These are not distractions. They are medicine.

> *"Life will not always give you big reasons to keep going. Sometimes, you must notice the small ones."*

Her story reminds us of a powerful truth: sometimes, the will to live is sparked by something as small as the smell of a pineapple. And when that lit, it can defy even the darkest odds. Just as relationships can be vessels of healing or harm, so too can our inner world shape our physical health. Our emotional imbalances — desire, rage, pride — don't stay confined to the mind. They trickle into our bodies, weakening immunity, fueling inflammation, and silently laying the foundation for illness. It is here that the worlds of inner peace and outer vitality collide.

She just made a formula that could save her life — and maybe yours.

It's called 'The MEDSRX Way' — a life prescription to strengthen your body, calm your mind, and protect your soul against cancer and the silent creep of lifestyle diseases. This isn't just a checklist. It's a way of living that reclaims your health from the inside out.

M for Meditation – ***Calm the mind, center the soul.***

Every day, spend 25–30 minutes in quiet stillness or guided meditation. Feel your breath steady, your thoughts soften, your spirit settle. This is your daily meeting with yourself.

- **What it is:** A practice of mindfulness, stillness, or focused awareness that lowers stress and clears the mental fog.
- **How to do it:** Breath-focused meditation, body scans, gentle visualization, mantras, or mindful moments while walking or cooking.
- **Why it matters:** Increases clarity, emotional balance, creativity, and the inner resilience to face life head-on.

E for Exercise – ***Move your body, energize your life.***

Your body is built to move. Dedicate 30–45 minutes daily to walking, dancing, yoga, running, or swimming. Each heartbeat during movement is a drumbeat of vitality.

- **What it is:** Physical activity that fuels strength, stamina, and flexibility.
- **How to do it:** Choose what you enjoy — walking under open skies, lifting weights, stretching into yoga poses, or splashing in the pool.
- **Why it matters:** Improves mood, strengthens immunity, enhances brain health, and makes every part of you feel more alive.

D for Diet – ***Fuel your body with intention.***

Your gut is your second brain — treat it with love. Choose whole, plant-rich foods. Avoid heavy, oily, over-processed meals that drain your energy. Think vibrant colors on your plate: greens, reds, oranges, and purples.

- **What it is:** Giving your body the nutrition it craves, not just the calories it needs.
- **How to do it:** Fill your meals with vegetables, fruits, grains, lean proteins, and healthy fats. Drink enough water.
- **Why it matters:** Enhances energy, strengthens immunity, improves mood, and supports long-term health.

S for Sleep – *Rest deeply to rise fully.*

Sleep is not laziness; it's sacred repair time. In 7–9 hours of uninterrupted rest, your body heals, your mind resets, and your soul finds quiet.

- **What it is:** A nightly recharge for every cell in your body.
- **How to do it:** Keep a consistent sleep schedule, avoid screens before bed, and create a calm environment.
- **Why it matters:** Improves memory, emotional stability, hormonal balance, and physical recovery.

R for Relationship & Relaxation – *Connect deeply, live fully.*

We heal faster and live longer when we are loved, supported, and understood. Invest in the people who uplift you and release those who drain you. And give yourself permission to pause, laugh, and breathe.

- **What it is:** A blend of human connection and restorative stillness.

- **How to do it:** Practice honesty, empathy, and active listening. Spend time with people who inspire joy and trust.
- **Why it matters:** Reduces stress, increases happiness, and weaves you into a network of emotional strength.

X for X-Factor – *Your unique spark.*

This is your reason to leap out of bed in the morning. A passion, a cause, an adventure — whatever lights up your soul. It's not extra; it's essential.

- **What it is:** The purpose, passion, or creative force that keeps you thriving.
- **How to do it:** Explore art, music, writing, teaching, traveling, volunteering, learning — anything that makes you feel more *you*.
- **Why it matters:** Boosts motivation, builds resilience, and gives life depth and joy.

When all six work together, something magical happens:

- You become more resilient in hard times.
- Your body feels lighter, stronger, and more alive.
- Your mind clears; your decisions sharpen.
- Your relationships deepen.
- You rediscover joy — both in the company of others and in your own presence.

Cancer's true healing begins long before medicine — it starts with how we live, love, think, and connect. The MEDSRX Formula is not just about avoiding illness; it's about choosing a life of wholeness. When we nourish our body, discipline our mind, express our emotions, sleep with peace, build healthy relationships, and stay spiritually grounded, we become our own best caretakers.

Cancer may attack the body, but a life lived consciously and lovingly can fortify the soul. Prevention is not simply a physical effort — it's a holistic commitment to self-care, self-respect, and self-awareness.

In the end, your lifestyle is your greatest medicine. Choose wisely, live intentionally, and protect your inner light — because your life isn't just meant to be survived, it's meant to be deeply lived.

It is not the body alone that bears disease, but the soul burdened with unexpressed pain and unhealed wounds.

CHAPTER TWO

The Foundations of a Lasting Relationship

The Role of Honesty in Human Relationships

Human beings are inherently social. Whether it's with family, friends, romantic partners, colleagues, or even pets, relationships form the emotional foundation of our lives. They give us strength, support, and inspiration to overcome life's many challenges.

At the core of any lasting relationship is honesty. Without it, even the strongest bond can erode over time. Being honest isn't just about telling the truth; it's about being open, sincere, and transparent. It's about creating a space where both individuals can be themselves, share their truths, and build trust.

A Story of Shared Truth

I once knew a couple who each carried a painful secret. The man was sterile and feared losing his partner if he told her. Unknown to him, she too had struggled silently—unable to conceive due to a past ovarian tumor. After months of uncertainty, they finally sat down and shared their truths. With tears of relief, they embraced a new path forward and decided to adopt. Their honesty didn't break the relationship—it strengthened it, laying the foundation for a marriage rooted in trust.

When Honesty is Hard: My Own Personal Journey

Seventeen years.

That's how long my marriage lasted—a whole era of my life, painted in every color of the emotional spectrum: the golden warmth of love, the bright sparkle of laughter, the soft glow of hope… and the deep shadows of heartbreak.

Like many love stories, ours began in a haze of promise. We whispered dreams into the night and held hands with the quiet certainty that we had found *our person*. We built what we believed was a solid home—its foundation laid with honesty, trust, respect, and open communication.

But here's the truth I only fully understood later: even the strongest structures can weaken—not always with a single earthquake, but with the slow, almost invisible settling of the ground beneath them.

It started subtly. A truth left unspoken here.
A misunderstanding left to fade instead of being untangled.
The comfortable silences we once cherished stretched into long, uneasy gaps. Small disappointments were folded neatly into the back corners of our hearts, hidden away… until they quietly became walls between us.

I still ask myself: Was it pride? Was it fear? Or was it sheer emotional fatigue that made honesty harder to come by? Because honesty, while noble, is not always easy. Sometimes it invites conflict we'd rather avoid. Sometimes it demands that we show our deepest vulnerabilities. And sometimes… it forces us to face truths we're not ready to see.

So instead of speaking, we stayed silent.

We tried to repair the cracks through late-night conversations, family trips, and even professional counseling. But by then, the fractures ran too deep. The bond we once thought indestructible had grown thin, fragile, and quiet. And in the end, despite nearly two decades of shared memories, we let go.

I've learned my story is far from unique. Marriage itself is changing. Divorce rates are rising—not just in the West, but also in countries like India, where marriage was once considered a lifelong pact, often kept regardless of personal happiness. Today, social taboos have loosened. Women have greater financial independence. People are more willing to step away from relationships that no longer nurture them.

But cultural change is only part of the story. Modern life has its own invisible knives—long work hours, the endless hum of technology, financial pressures, and the fading of traditional support systems. Once, extended families and close-knit communities offered couples a safety net. Now, many stand in the storm alone.

Looking back, I don't see my marriage as a failure. I see it as a chapter—full of joy, mistakes, resilience, and no doubt lessons. It taught me that love is not just an emotion. Love is a choice—one we have to make, over and over again. And honesty? That's the oxygen that choice needs to survive. Without it, connection thins… and eventually, love struggles to breathe.

This is my story. But it's also a reflection of countless others walking the same delicate path. Because while every relationship is unique, the struggles with honesty, trust, respect, and communication are universal. And perhaps the greatest relationship skill we can ever learn is this: to face those struggles early, before the small cracks turn into chasms.

Lessons I Learned About Honesty in Relationships:

1. Honesty is not just about facts—it's about feelings.
   Being truthful doesn't only mean avoiding lies. It means sharing your emotional reality, even when it feels uncomfortable.
2. Silence can be more damaging than a difficult truth.
   What goes unsaid doesn't just disappear; it often grows into resentment or misunderstanding.
3. Honesty requires courage—and practice.
   We often avoid being honest because we fear the other person's reaction. But honesty, like trust, is built through small, consistent acts.
4. You can't control how the other person responds—but you can control your integrity.
   Speaking your truth with kindness preserves your self-respect, even if the outcome isn't what you hoped.
5. If honesty is lost, work on it immediately.
   Avoiding the issue only deepens the cracks. Addressing it early can prevent irreversible damage.
6. Sometimes honesty means letting go.
   Being true to yourself may mean ending a relationship that no longer aligns with your values, needs, or well-being.

Though my marriage ended, my belief in love did not. I've learned that endings are not always tragedies—they can be gateways to new beginnings. Honesty may be hard, but it is also freeing. It allows you to live without the weight of pretense, to open your heart again without fear, and to rebuild a life rooted in truth. Sometimes the bravest thing we can do is to be honest—with others, and with ourselves—and trust that whatever comes next will be worth the courage it took to get there.

The Relationship Crisis in Modern Times

Today's world presents countless stressors:

- Work-related pressures
- Financial uncertainty
- Lack of quality time
- Overuse of technology and social media
- Emotional fatigue

These stressors often lead to:

- Decreased intimacy
- Increased conflict
- Emotional distance
- Lowered satisfaction in relationships

How to Strengthen Relationships

There are practical, evidence-based ways to nurture and strengthen relationships:

1. **Open Communication**: Share openly without fear of judgment. Listen actively and express yourself honestly.
2. **Stress Management**: Engage in practices like meditation, yoga, or mindfulness. Sometimes professional therapy is necessary.
3. **Quality Time**: Prioritize meaningful time together to foster intimacy and connection.

4. **Seek Help When Needed**: Don't hesitate to approach a counselor or therapist.
5. **Set Healthy Boundaries**: Keep work and personal lives balanced and protect the privacy of your relationship.
6. **Problem-Focused Coping**: Address root causes directly and work together to find solutions.
7. **Mutual Support**: Be present for each other's challenges, offering empathy and encouragement.

Honesty: The Cornerstone of Connection

The proverb "Honesty is the best policy" isn't just moral advice—it's practical. Honesty builds credibility, nurtures respect, and forms the foundation for lasting bonds. Whether in friendships, work relationships, or marriage, being truthful allows us to be seen and accepted for who we truly are.

Take the example of Lal Bahadur Shastri, India's former Prime Minister. Despite his high position, he lived modestly and within his means. When he couldn't afford a saree for his wife, he refused a shopkeeper's offer to take it for free, reminding us that integrity begins in the small moments.

The Danger of "Small Lies"

So-called "white lies" may seem harmless, but over time, they erode trust. Examples include:

- Saying "I'm fine" when you're not
- Promising to call back but not intending to
- Claiming you didn't receive a message
- Blaming traffic for being late when that's not the truth

These lies create a pattern of dishonesty, emotional distance, and self-doubt. Eventually, they damage the very foundation of a relationship.

Extraordinary Stories of Love and Commitment

True love can endure through incredible circumstances. Some couples are separated by war, marry others, and reconnect decades later to remarry. In one case, a man with dementia forgot his wife, proposed to her again, and they remarried—a beautiful testimony to enduring love and devotion.

In today's world of speed, constant comparison, and the lure of convenience, your mindset is either your greatest asset—or your biggest limitation.

If you're aiming for clarity, success, and a life of deeper meaning, it all begins with shaping the way you think. And the way you think is molded—not in grand gestures, but in the small habits you live by every day.

Here are **three powerful habits** that can rewire your thinking and unlock a happier, more purposeful life:

1. Practice Delayed Gratification

Temptations are everywhere—gadgets, sales, sugary snacks, impulsive buys. But before you reach for them, pause. Ask yourself: *Do I truly need this—or just want it now?*

When you learn to delay gratification, you're not depriving yourself—you're training your mind to value what matters. It strengthens decision-making and builds long-term self-respect.

Over time, this one habit makes you feel more in control of your life.

2. Eat with Awareness

We often eat while scrolling, watching, or rushing. But food is not just fuel—it's an experience that connects your body and mind.

When you eat with full attention—savoring each bite—you not only digest food better but also become more present in life. Mindful eating becomes a practice of gratitude, discipline, and self-connection.

3. Step Outside Your Comfort Zone (Lovingly)

Your comfort zone may feel safe, but it's not where growth happens. Every moment of discomfort holds the seed of strength.

Learn to love the challenge, even if it's uncomfortable. Whether it's speaking up, learning something new, or facing your fears—each step outside your comfort zone builds resilience, courage, and character.

In the end, the secret to a better life isn't found in tools, talent, money, or even time.

It's found in one thing:

👉A better mindset.

And a better mindset is not born overnight—it is built slowly, patiently—day by day, habit by habit.

Choose your habits wisely. They become the bricks of the life you're creating.

What Makes a Relationship Healthy?

While relationships vary, healthy ones are built on:

- **Honest and open communication**
- **Healthy boundaries**
- **Mutual respect**
- **Emotional and practical support**

Such relationships are key to both mental and physical well-being. People in strong relationships:

- **Live longer**
- **Experience lower depression and anxiety**
- **Have higher self-esteem**
- **Feel a greater sense of purpose**

Each of us has a story where the kindness of truth and the strength of love make the invisible visible. In relationships, it isn't perfection that sustains love—it's honesty, resilience, and the willingness to grow together.

Relationship Self-Reflection Quiz

Consider these statements to reflect on your relationship. Use a scale of 1 (Strongly Disagree) to 5 (Strongly Agree):

1. It's fine for my partner to read my personal emails.
2. My partner and I are a good match.
3. Keeping secrets from my partner won't hurt.

4. Our relationship is a good model for others.
5. I'd rather suffer than let my partner suffer.
6. I trust my partner not to cheat.
7. I want to see my partner beside me every morning.
8. We talk about even small matters.
9. We prefer spending time together over others.
10. Physical and emotional closeness matters to us.
11. We support each other's personal goals.
12. We consistently appreciate each other.
13. We speak in terms of "we" and "us."
14. Our relationship is mostly happy and positive.
15. We are committed to a long-term bond.
16. We respect each other despite differences.
17. We support each other in good and bad times.
18. We resolve problems peacefully.
19. We encourage personal and professional growth.
20. We confide in each other during important moments.

CHAPTER THREE

Building trust through Relationships

Rebuilding Trust: The Foundation of Strong Relationships

Trust is the cornerstone of all meaningful relationships—whether personal, professional, or communal. It is not handed out freely but earned through consistent, honest, and dependable actions over time. At its core, trust is built by demonstrating integrity, empathy, transparency, openness to feedback, and the courage to admit mistakes.

Earning trust requires vulnerability and effort. It demands that we show others they matter, that we value our shared connection enough to nurture it. Each decision, conversation, and honest moment adds to a growing foundation of mutual respect. Whether forming trust in a new relationship or rebuilding it after a breach, the process is always intentional and deeply personal.

What Is Trust?

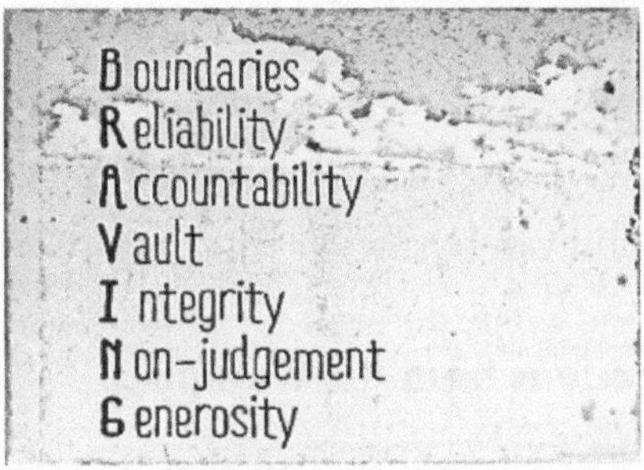

Source: Wallpapers.com

If you struggle with trust issues or are working to restore broken trust, this article is for you. It explores the core concepts, rituals, and mindset shifts necessary to build and sustain trust.

Trust is central to every form of human interaction. To trust someone means to feel safe, understood, and valued in their presence. Equally important is being trustworthy ourselves. Research shows that interpersonal trust has declined significantly in recent decades, making trust-building even more critical today.

There are two main dimensions of trust:

- **Practical Trust**: Built on reliability, consistency, and accountability.
- **Emotional Trust**: Rooted in empathy, compassion, and emotional intelligence.

To cultivate trust, we must honor our commitments, admit our mistakes, communicate clearly, express vulnerability, stand by our values, and demonstrate genuine care. Trust is a long-term process requiring daily attention.

A story from the *Ramayana* highlights this beautifully. When Hanuman first met Sita in Ashoka Vatika, he didn't immediately rescue her. First, he had to earn her trust by showing respect and sharing information only she would recognize. This moment underscores how trust must be established before meaningful help or connection can occur.

Real-Life Reflections from the Workplace

While writing *Beyond Physical Romance*, I realized that trust in the workplace is not merely a nice-to-have—it is the invisible current that shapes relationships, productivity, and morale. Over the years, as a CEO, I've learned that effective leadership is about shifting the focus from *"I"* to *"you."* It's about listening before speaking, serving before expecting, and making decisions that honor both people and purpose.

I have found that true leadership is not just about strategy or results—it is about being present, accessible, and genuinely invested in those you lead. My goal has always been to lead with empathy, to be approachable no matter the circumstance, and to ensure my team knows that my door—and my mind—are always open.

Trust in a Moment of Crisis

One afternoon, I received a hesitant knock on my office door. It was Priya, one of our most dedicated project managers. Her usual confident smile was gone; instead, her eyes brimmed with tears.

"Do you have a minute?" she asked, her voice trembling.

She sat down and, after a deep breath, confessed that she had sent an incorrect file to one of our biggest clients. The error had already caused confusion in the client's team and could potentially delay a high-stakes project. She was certain I would be furious—or worse, that her job was on the line.

I could see the fear in her body language, but I also saw something else: the courage it took for her to come to me directly. She trusted that she could be honest, even when it was risky.

Instead of reacting with anger, I leaned forward and said, "Thank you for telling me right away. Let's figure this out together."

Her shoulders relaxed instantly. We walked through the details step-by-step, crafted a recovery plan, and I personally called the client to explain the situation and assure them it would be resolved. The matter was closed within hours, not days.

But what mattered most was not that we fixed the mistake quickly—it was that the experience deepened our working relationship. Priya told me later that my reaction made her feel more loyal to the company than ever before, because she knew she was valued as a person, not just as a performer.

Building Trust from Scratch

When I first met Arjun, he had been with the company for just two weeks. A talented software developer, he had joined from a smaller firm where the culture was strict and punitive. In his previous role, employees were discouraged from speaking up, and mistakes were met with public reprimand.

In his third week, Arjun missed a project deadline due to a coding error that took longer than expected to fix. He avoided my calls and emails, clearly expecting the worst. When I finally met him in person, I noticed how tense he was—shoulders hunched, eyes downcast.

I began the conversation with something unexpected: "Arjun, I'm glad you're here. Let's talk about what happened, not to blame you, but to see how we can make sure you have what you need to succeed."

He looked up in surprise. "You're… not angry?" he asked, almost disbelieving.

I shook my head. "Deadlines matter, but your growth matters more. We'll work together on this."

Over the next few months, I made it a point to check in with him regularly—not to monitor him, but to mentor him. I encouraged him to speak openly in team meetings, praised his innovative solutions, and gave him opportunities to lead small projects. Slowly, the guardedness faded. By the end of the year, Arjun was not only delivering his work on time but also mentoring junior developers.

Later, he told me something that stayed with me: *"I didn't think I'd ever trust a boss again. But you changed that."*

The Ongoing Work of Trust

Trust in the workplace is not formed in a single conversation; it is built brick by brick, through everyday actions. I make it a priority to know my team members as people, not just job titles—learning about their families, dreams, challenges, and strengths. I write handwritten thank-you notes to acknowledge their contributions. I give thoughtful gifts that reflect their personalities. I check in often—not just when something goes wrong, but to celebrate small wins and ask how they're doing.

Mentorship has also been one of the most rewarding parts of my career. I've guided countless interns, fresh graduates, and even the children of friends who are navigating early professional challenges. My first question is always the same: *"Would you like me to listen, or would you like me to give advice?"* That simple choice hands them agency over the conversation and shows that I value their comfort as much as their growth.

Leadership, at its heart, is a relationship built on trust. It's not about holding authority—it's about holding space. And when trust is the anchor, teams don't just follow a leader; they walk alongside them.

Rebuilding Trust: The Story of the Cracked Vase

Restoring broken trust takes time, patience, and emotional effort. While the relationship may never return to its original form, it can evolve into something even stronger.

Let me share a story that captures this idea:

The Cracked Vase

Neelam gently turned the key to her mother's house. Eight months had passed since she last visited—eight long months of silence and sorrow.

She had sold her mother's heirloom vase, a treasured family artifact, without permission. Facing financial ruin, Neelam acted in desperation, hoping to recover it later. But her mother discovered the truth, and the sense of betrayal ran deep.

Now, Neelam returned with the vase—not in perfect condition, but lovingly restored using golden lacquer in the Japanese art of kintsugi. This method doesn't hide cracks; it celebrates them as part of an object's history.

"I bought it back," she said quietly. "I didn't cover the cracks. I want you to see them."

Her mother traced the golden seams with her fingers and whispered, "Your grandmother believed that broken things could still carry love."

With tears in her eyes, Neelam asked, "Can we carry ours?"

Her mother replied, "If we keep mending, then yes."

It wasn't a perfect reunion, but it was a new beginning.

This story reminds us that relationships are not defined by perfection, but by our willingness to repair and renew them with honesty and humility.

Trust: The Bedrock of Leadership and Life

Trust is the silent architecture of every successful relationship in the world. It allows us to take emotional risks, seek support, and grow together. Leadership, teamwork, and intimacy all depend on trust.

It doesn't develop overnight. It takes vulnerability, empathy, and initiative. But once established, trust creates the space for healing, growth, and deeper connection.

When Did You Last Feel Trusted?

Just think about it: When was the last time someone fully trusted you—or you trusted someone else? Not the casual kind of trust, like lending someone a pen, but the deep, soul-level trust where you know they have your back no matter what. How did it make you feel? Empowered? Brave? Truly seen?

Trust is one of the earliest lessons we learn in life. As infants, we cry not out of manipulation but instinct, expecting that someone will come. Each time a parent picks us up, we begin to form an invisible thread of security: *I am safe. My needs matter.* As we grow, that thread is woven by parents, siblings, teachers, friends, colleagues, and mentors.

But threads can fray. A broken promise from a parent, a betrayal from a friend, or an authority figure who abuses their position can teach us to guard ourselves. Some of us respond by becoming fiercely self-reliant—hyper-independent—not out of true strength, but because we fear that relying on others will lead to disappointment or pain.

That's why self-trust is so vital. It is the anchor from which all other trust flows. When we believe in our ability to make good choices, recover from mistakes, and stay true to ourselves, we approach relationships from a place of strength, not desperation. Self-trust means knowing that even if others let us down, we will not abandon ourselves at any cost.

And yet, something remarkable happens when trust flows both ways. When someone looks us in the eye and says, "I believe in you," a quiet shift occurs. Their faith becomes a mirror, reflecting a version of ourselves we might not yet see. It invites us to take risks, to step into roles we never imagined, to rise to challenges with courage.

A story of trust:

When Rina was 23, she got her first job as a junior graphic designer. Three months in, her manager handed her the lead role on a high-profile project after the senior designer quit unexpectedly.

"Are you sure?" she asked, panic creeping in. "I've never led anything this big before."

Her manager smiled. "I trust you. You've got the eye, the skill, and the heart for it. Now show them what you can do."

In that moment, Rina felt a strange mixture of fear and exhilaration. Someone believed in her more than she believed in herself. She worked late nights, taught herself new tools, and pulled the team together. The campaign was a success—and Rina realized something important: her manager's trust had unlocked a part of her she didn't know existed.

Trust, whether given or received, is not just a bond—it's a catalyst for growth, believe me. It transforms fear into possibilities and doubt into determination.

Self-Trust Evaluation

Take a moment to reflect on the following statements. Answer Yes or No:

1. ___ I often put others' needs ahead of my own.
2. ___ I feel ashamed of my difficult emotions like anger or sadness.
3. ___ I frequently feel something is wrong with me.
4. ___ I doubt my own abilities despite praise from others.
5. ___ I hide my mistakes out of fear.
6. ___ I find it hard to ask for help.
7. ___ I am uncomfortable discussing money or success.
8. ___ I believe others are more honest than I am.
9. ___ I fear failure when pursuing big goals.
10. ___ I worry I'll fail competitive exams or tasks.
11. ___ I trust that I have strengths and good qualities.
12. ___ I avoid criticism or feedback.
13. ___ I dwell more on my flaws than on my strengths.

14. ___ I rarely question my decisions and think I'm always right.
15. ___ I often compare myself to more confident people.
16. ___ I defer to others' opinions over my own.
17. ___ I struggle to recognize and prioritize my desires.
18. ___ I expect failure before I even begin something.
19. ___ I don't always keep promises or commitments.
20. ___ I hold onto past resentment and anger.

Reflect on your responses. The more "Yes" answers you gave to self-affirming questions and "No" to self-doubting ones, the stronger your self-trust likely is.

CHAPTER FOUR

Importance of Respect and Boundaries

Respect is crucial for fostering positive relationships, healthy communication, and a harmonious society. It involves acknowledging the value and worth of others, treating them with dignity, and valuing their opinions and feelings. Showing respect creates a more inclusive environment, reduces conflict, and boosts self-esteem for both the giver and the receiver.

(Source: WallPapers.com)

Honoring Self-Respect and Boundaries

Practicing self-respect and honoring boundaries begins with understanding your own needs, emotions, and limits—while also valuing those of others. It means setting clear, healthy boundaries in every area of life—emotional, physical, mental, and social—and communicating them with confidence and clarity.

Boundaries are not about building walls; they are about creating safe spaces where both you and others can thrive. When you honor your own boundaries, you affirm your self-worth and protect your well-being. When you respect the boundaries of others, you nurture trust, empathy, and mutual respect.

I've always found comfort in consistency, living a life guided by a steady rhythm. Yet when it comes to travel, I rarely visit the same place twice—new places bring fresh perspectives and unexpected adventures with new, unknown knowledge. Still, there are moments of unease, like walking into an unfamiliar land without clear markers. Is it a public path, a private garden, or a farmer's field? That hesitation—the uncertainty of where you stand—mirrors what life feels like without boundaries.

A boundary, much like a signpost, marks the limits. It tells us where we are, where we can go, and where we shouldn't. Without clear boundaries or open communication, it's easy to lose our way. Boundaries offer clarity, structure, and safety. They don't confine; they define.

Setting boundaries with others is vital and crucial, but so is setting them with ourselves. Personal boundaries protect our goals, values, and emotional health. They serve as internal guideposts, helping us stay aligned with our priorities and uphold our standards. If you often struggle to keep commitments to yourself or feel overwhelmed by the demands of others, it may be time to strengthen your boundaries.

The first obstacle to living within your boundaries is not having them clearly defined. Without them, it's easy to overextend, neglect your needs, and compromise your well-being. A strong mind–body connection can help you recognize when something feels wrong and trust your intuition to guide you.

Boundaries are not barriers; they are bridges to confidence, intention, and self-respect. They protect your energy, time, and emotional balance, allowing you to show up more authentically in your relationships, responsibilities, and life as a whole.

Honoring and Practicing Boundaries

By formulating and honoring your own boundaries, you can:

- Increase self-respect and confidence – Knowing and expressing your limits affirms your self-worth and encourages others to treat you with respect.
- Improve focus and productivity – Clear boundaries help you prioritize what truly matters and avoid unnecessary distractions.
- Enhance mental and physical health – Saying "no" when necessary reduces stress, anxiety, and burnout.
- Strengthen relationships – Healthy limits promote mutual respect and prevent resentment, misunderstandings, and emotional fatigue.

Setting boundaries is not selfish—it's an essential form of self-care.

When you live in alignment with your values and needs, you create space for healthier, more fulfilling connections—with others and with yourself.

Start Small and Be Specific:

When people think of "boundaries," they imagine massive life changes—quitting jobs, cutting off relationships, moving to new cities. But boundaries often start much smaller.

When I was in my first year as an Automotive Engineer, I had a colleague who would call me at 10 or 11 p.m. for "quick help." At first, I answered every time, thinking I was being a team player. But my sleep suffered, my mornings became rushed, and my mood was constantly sour.

One day, I simply told him: *"I'll help with anything urgent until 7 p.m., but after that, I'm offline."* The first time I said it, my voice trembled. But within a week, something amazing happened—I was sleeping better, my evenings felt lighter, and my productivity the next day improved.

Takeaway: Your first boundary might be as small as choosing when you answer calls. But small boundaries, applied consistently, create big shifts in your well-being.

Boundaries Protect Your Best Self

As a son and brother, I've always wanted to be available for my family. But there was a period when I was constantly saying yes—to errands, favors, and last-minute plans—even when I was exhausted after work.

I remember one Sunday when I had planned to rest and finish a personal project, but I ended up driving all over town helping a cousin. I didn't resent helping him, but I did resent the fact that I didn't even ask myself if I *could* say no.

Eventually, I started communicating my limits: *"I can help, but I'll need to do it after my own commitments are done."* Surprisingly, my family respected it—and even started asking how *I* was doing before requesting help.

Takeaway: Boundaries are not walls—they're filters. They don't keep love out; they protect the energy that allows you to give it freely.

Boundaries Build Mutual Respect

When you consistently express your limits, you teach people how to treat you.

A close friend of mine had a habit of sending me long voice messages during my busiest work hours. I used to stop what I was doing to listen and reply because I didn't want her to think I was ignoring her. But my focus at work suffered, and I began to feel drained by our conversations.

So, I explained: *"I really value our chats, but I can only listen after work hours so I can be fully present for you."* Not only did she understand, but she also admitted she'd been feeling guilty for interrupting my work time. Our conversations became richer—because they happened when I could give her my full attention.

Boundaries show others that your time and presence are valuable—and that you respect theirs too.

Boundaries Improve, Not Destroy, Relationships

At first, I worried that setting boundaries would push people away. But over time, I've found the opposite: my relationships have become more honest and sustainable.

When I told a project partner that I couldn't take on extra tasks because I needed weekends for rest, I braced for disappointment. Instead, he said, *"I should do the same. I've been burning out too."* That conversation not only improved our workflow but also strengthened our trust in each other.

Boundaries often inspire others to set their own—creating healthier dynamics all around.

Boundaries Are a Practice, Not a One-Time Act

I'm still learning to set boundaries, and each time I do, they become clearer and easier to uphold. Some days, I slip back into old habits of overcommitting. But I remind myself that boundaries are like muscles—they get stronger the more you use them.

I would say that boundaries are not acts of selfishness; they are acts of stewardship over your own life. They protect the clarity, energy, and joy that make you capable of showing up fully for yourself and for the people who matter most. Boundaries also teach others how to treat us. They communicate self-respect and invite mutual respect. They're about knowing your limits, expressing them with kindness, and staying consistent even when it's uncomfortable.

Lessons I've learnt About Boundaries:

- Start small – You don't need to overhaul your life overnight. Begin with one area where you feel overwhelmed or taken for granted.
- Be clear and kind – Communicate your boundaries calmly and confidently.
- Expect resistance – Not everyone will understand or support your choices, and that's okay.
- Stick to your limits – Boundaries lose their power if they're not reinforced.

The more I prioritize my needs, the more energy I have for the people and activities that truly matter. Boundaries are not walls—they're bridges to a healthier, more grounded version of myself. As I continue to learn and grow, I hope to inspire others to do the same.

Wisdom from *Boundaries* by Henry Cloud & John Townsend:

- "We have our own thoughts, and if we want others to know them, we must tell them."
- "To rescue people from the natural consequences of their behavior is to render them powerless."
- "Forgiveness gives me boundaries because it unhooks me from the hurtful person, and then I can act responsibly and

wisely. If I am not forgiving them, I am still in a destructive relationship with them."

Insights from *Boundaries* by Anne Katherine:

- "When a person neither knows his feelings nor has healthy ways to handle them, he is vulnerable to whatever will keep his feelings contained—alcohol or other drugs, food, excessive work, stress, compulsive acquiring, compulsive hobbying."
- "We have spiritual boundaries. You are the only one who knows the right spiritual path for yourself. If someone tries to tell you he knows the only way you can believe, he's out of line."
- "A wife is not the best person to teach her husband how to feel."

Setting Boundaries: A Path to Peace and Self-Respect

Setting boundaries is not about shutting people out—it's about creating the space for genuine connection, self-respect, and inner peace. This peace emerges from a journey of self-discovery, self-compassion, and self-love. Boundaries protect your emotional, mental, and physical energy. They keep you aligned with your values, help you stay in control of your time, and ensure that your commitments reflect what truly matters to you.

When you communicate your needs clearly and respectfully, you're not being selfish—you're prioritizing your well-being and nurturing healthier, more respectful relationships. Boundaries are not barriers to connection; they are bridges to mutual understanding, emotional safety, and authentic living. They allow you to feel less overwhelmed, more grounded, and deeply in tune with your inner voice. Their positive impact extends into every part of life—family, friendships, work, and, most importantly, your relationship with yourself.

Learning to set and honor boundaries is a powerful act of self-respect. It's a declaration that your needs, feelings, and values matter. Though uncomfortable at first, each step you take toward clarity brings you closer to a life rooted in peace, purpose, and authenticity. As your self-awareness grows, you'll see that boundaries are not just self-care—they're a gift you give both yourself and those you connect with meaningfully.

Respect and boundaries are not abstract concepts; they're values forged through lived experience. I once believed that saying "yes" was a sign of kindness—a way to be liked or to do the right thing. But in trying to meet everyone's expectations, I stretched myself thin. I ignored the quiet signals of fatigue, irritability, and resentment. Then came the realization: respect for others should never come at the cost of disrespecting myself.

Boundaries are not walls—they are doors with clear signs. They welcome in what nourishes you and keep out what drains you. They shape how you engage with the world and, in turn, how the world engages with you.

In personal relationships, I've witnessed how unspoken expectations and ignored boundaries breed misunderstandings and heartache. But I've also seen the healing that happens when we speak up—with honesty and compassion. A simple "no" or "I need space" can be an act of courage and love.

In my professional life, boundaries have protected me from burnout, allowed me to focus on what truly matters, and created space for respectful, collaborative partnerships. I've learned that respect must be mutual—and it begins with self-respect. When we uphold our boundaries, we teach others how to treat us, showing that we are worthy of dignity, care, and understanding.

Boundaries are not isolation—they are protection for what matters most: your time, energy, and peace of mind. They invite connection rather than conflict, allowing us to show up in the world confident, grounded, and respected.

Through my own journey, I've come to see boundaries not as restrictions but as vital acts of self-respect. They bring clarity, peace, and authenticity to our lives. Honoring them isn't a one-time choice—it's a daily practice, rooted in self-awareness and reinforced by the decisions we make.

Life teaches us its importance, sometimes through the discomfort of giving too much, and other times through the empowerment that comes from saying "enough." In friendships, boundaries mean the freedom to say "no" without guilt and to voice your needs without fear. In families, they mean respecting privacy and individuality. In romantic relationships, they are the foundation of trust and intimacy, allowing both partners to feel safe, valued, and free to be themselves.

When you honor your boundaries, you honor your worth—and that, more than anything, is the key to living with peace, purpose, and connection.

Honoring Boundaries for a Balanced, Authentic Life

In my professional life, honoring boundaries has been the key to avoiding burnout and focusing on what truly matters. It has helped me set realistic goals, maintain a healthier work–life balance, and build respectful, collaborative relationships.

I've learned that respect must be mutual—but it begins with self-respect. When we value ourselves enough to define and uphold our boundaries, we teach others how to treat us. We show them that we are worthy of dignity, care, and understanding.

Boundaries are not walls meant to keep people out—they are protective frameworks that safeguard your time, energy, and peace of mind. When you clearly communicate your needs and limits, you invite deeper trust, openness, and honesty. Healthy boundaries strengthen connection rather than weaken it. They allow us to show up fully—confident, grounded, and respected—in every part of our lives.

Through personal experience, I've come to see boundaries not as restrictions, but as essential acts of self-respect. They bring clarity, calm, and authenticity to both relationships and daily life. Honoring them is not a one-time choice—it's a daily practice, rooted in self-awareness and reinforced with each decision we make. The more we live by them, the more empowered and connected we feel—to ourselves and to the world around us.

Boundaries are the invisible lines that protect our emotional, mental, and physical well-being. They define what is acceptable to us and what isn't, guiding both how we treat others and how we allow others to treat us. Sometimes we learn their importance the hard way—by overextending ourselves, feeling drained, or allowing too much access to our time and emotions. Other times, we witness how setting clear limits transforms our relationships for the better.

Examples of Boundaries in Action:

- **Friendships:** Having the space to say "no" without guilt and the freedom to express your needs openly.
- **Families:** Respecting privacy, emotional space, and personal independence.
- **Romantic Relationships:** Creating trust and intimacy by ensuring both partners feel safe, valued, and heard.
- **Workplace:** Saying "no" to after-hours demands and setting clear expectations with colleagues to preserve energy and productivity.

Visual Symbols of Healthy Boundaries:

- A person calmly stepping back during a heated conversation—signifying emotional space.
- A door slightly ajar with a "Do Not Disturb" sign—representing the need for personal time.
- Two people sitting together on a bench, facing in different directions—showing individuality within togetherness.
- A person holding a "No" sign with a warm smile—asserting limits kindly.

- A circle drawn in sand around someone—symbolizing self-protection and personal space.

Boundaries are not about distance; they are about clarity. They help us let the right people in, in the right way. Practicing them deepens our self-respect and encourages healthier, more fulfilling relationships. A boundary is not a barrier—it's a bridge to balanced, authentic living.

Self-Reflection Quiz: How Well Do You Maintain and Respect Boundaries?

Answer Yes or No:

1. I say "no" when I genuinely cannot take on more responsibilities.
2. I feel guilty when I put my own needs before others'.
3. I clearly communicate my emotional, physical, and time boundaries to others.
4. I often agree to things just to avoid conflict, even when I don't want to.
5. I take time to reflect on what I am comfortable with and what I'm not.
6. I struggle to express discomfort when someone crosses a line.
7. I make space in my life for rest, personal time, and self-care.
8. I expect others to automatically understand my needs without me stating them.
9. I feel safe and respected in most of my close relationships.
10. I find it difficult to deal with people who don't respect my boundaries.

11. I regularly check in with myself to see if my boundaries are being honored.
12. I can say "no" without over-explaining or justifying my decision.
13. I understand that others' disappointment is not my responsibility when I uphold my boundaries.
14. I feel empowered after asserting my limits.
15. I can recognize when someone is manipulating or guilt-tripping me into crossing my boundaries.
16. I give myself permission to walk away from situations or relationships that violate my boundaries.
17. I treat others' boundaries with the same respect I want for mine.
18. I reflect on past situations where I failed to set boundaries and use them as lessons.
19. I notice early warning signs of boundary crossing and act promptly.
20. I remind myself that setting boundaries is self-care, not selfishness.

Scoring Guide:

- Mostly Yes: You're actively maintaining healthy boundaries and honoring your well-being.
- Mix of Yes and No: You're aware of boundaries but may need more consistency.
- Mostly No: It's time to reflect on your limits and start setting stronger boundaries.

CHAPTER FIVE

Friendship and Relationship

Friendships and romantic relationships are two of life's most meaningful connections—each unique in nature, expectations, and the depth of intimacy they offer.

Friendships are often a calm, steady presence in our lives. They are platonic bonds we enter into by choice, built on mutual trust, shared experiences, and a sense of emotional safety. Friends are those we laugh with, confide in, and lean on during both ordinary days and life's storms. While deep and fulfilling, these relationships usually do not involve romantic or sexual feelings, allowing them to thrive in a space defined by companionship and understanding.

Romantic relationships, on the other hand, weave in additional layers—emotional and physical intimacy, romantic attraction, and often a stronger sense of exclusivity and long-term commitment. They may include dating, living together, or marriage, and often require a greater investment in communication, compromise, and conflict resolution. When nurtured well, they can bring profound joy, passion, and a sense of shared purpose.

Despite their differences, both friendships and romantic relationships rest upon the same essential pillars: honesty, trust, respect, and honest or open communication. Interestingly, they are not always fixed in form—friendships can blossom into romance, and romantic bonds can gracefully transition into friendships. The priority we give to each may shift throughout our lives, depending on personal circumstances, needs, and seasons of growth.

Together, friendships and romantic relationships shape our emotional world. They influence our well-being, help us discover more about ourselves, and enrich our journey through life.

Before you dive deeper into exploring these connections, take a moment for a short self-reflection quiz. It will help clarify your own perspectives and set the stage for a more insightful reading ahead.

Quiz: Friendships vs. Romantic Relationships

Part A: Multiple Choice

1. Which of the following is a key characteristic of a friendship?
    a) Romantic attraction
    b) Shared experiences and trust
    c) Legal commitment
    d) Exclusivity
2. What is usually expected in a romantic relationship but not in a typical friendship?

a) Respect
b) Emotional support
c) Commitment and intimacy
d) Communication

3. Friendships are generally:
   a) Involuntary and formal
   b) Based on romantic attraction
   c) Voluntary and platonic
   d) Secretive and temporary

4. Which of the following is more likely to involve conflict and the need for resolution strategies?
   a) Friendships
   b) Romantic relationships
   c) Acquaintanceships
   d) All of the above

Part B: True or False

5. Romantic relationships always begin as friendships.
   True / False

6. Both friendships and romantic relationships are built on trust, respect, and communication.
   True / False

7. It is not possible for a friendship to turn into a romantic relationship.
   True / False

8. People may value either friendships or romantic relationships more, depending on their life stage or circumstances.
   True / False

Part C: Short Answer

9. List two similarities between friendships and romantic relationships.

10. Name one way a friendship and a romantic relationship might evolve over time.

11. Why might romantic relationships require more conflict resolution than friendships

Strong, healthy relationships—whether romantic, family, or friendship—are vital to our happiness as human beings. Such relationships repair old connections and build meaningful new ones.

In today's hyper-connected world, it's easy to be deceived by numbers. My phone holds over 10,000 contacts—yet when life gets hard, that number becomes meaningless. Because true friendship isn't measured by how many people are on your list, but by who actually shows up when it matters most.

Friendship Day is not just about exchanging wishes or posting cheerful group photos online. It's not about parties, gifts, or fleeting fun. It's a quiet reminder of something rare and sacred—a relationship built not on convenience, but on presence. Unconditional, unwavering presence.

A real friend doesn't just "like" your updates. They notice your silences. They call when you go quiet. They stand by you not only when you're celebrating victories, but also when you're hurting, lost, or unsure of yourself. When the world looks away, they walk toward you.

Over the years, I've seen many people call themselves my friends—until I needed them. That's when I understood that friendship isn't about the many; it's about the few. The ones who remain when there's nothing to offer, nothing to gain.

So this Friendship Day, don't count your contacts. Count the ones who stayed. The ones who care quietly and stand beside you like a shadow, through every season of life. That's the kind of friendship worth celebrating.

Throughout my life, I've been in and out of relationships. Each one was different—shaped by its own unique emotions, challenges, and endings. Some faded quietly, others ended painfully. But through these experiences, especially the transitions from romantic to platonic (or the failure to do so), I've come to understand what real friendship means.

My first breakup was with my first girlfriend. When we parted ways, she accused me of not crying enough—not feeling enough. Maybe I looked too composed on the outside, but inside, I was still trying to make sense of it all. I didn't yet understand how to express the kind of loss I felt.

The next relationship led to marriage. But after a few years, the excitement and joy that had brought us together were slowly replaced by silence and distance. Her focus shifted entirely to money, and I pushed myself to the limit—working day and night in different countries just to keep her happy. I broke my back trying to provide, but I never saw a smile in return. I wouldn't call what we had a friendship. I felt more like a machine—a provider, nothing more.

Then came the second real breakup. We had been together for 17 years. I realized I was no longer in love with her, but what made the separation truly painful was losing the companionship we'd built. I didn't expect to cry, but I did. Because what I lost wasn't just a partner—it was a friend. A connection that had grown over time and had quietly become a part of me.

Looking back, I realize how vital communication is—not just in romantic relationships, but in all human connections. Honest, open, and regular communication could have made some of those transitions less painful and more meaningful. It could have helped preserve the friendship, even if the romance had to end.

In the end, I've learned that not every relationship will survive. But the ones rooted in genuine friendship stand the best chance of enduring—beyond love, beyond expectations, and even beyond separation.

While society often idealizes romantic relationships as the key to happiness, research shows that friendships are even more vital to our well-being. True friends bring joy, reduce stress, and help prevent loneliness.

Strong social connections aren't just good for the mind—they benefit the body too. Studies reveal that lacking friendships can be as harmful as smoking or a sedentary lifestyle, while maintaining close friendships may even increase lifespan.

However, meaningful friendships don't happen by chance. They require effort, time, and intention. Regardless of age or life stage, it's never too late to build or rebuild friendships—and doing so can significantly enhance your mental, emotional, and physical health.

Our society tends to place an emphasis on romantic relationships. We think that just finding the right person will make us happy and fulfilled. But research shows that friends are actually even more important to our psychological welfare. Friends bring more happiness into our lives than virtually anything else. Friendships have a huge impact on your mental health and happiness. Good friends relieve stress, provide comfort and joy, and prevent loneliness and isolation. Developing close friendships can also have a powerful impact on your physical health. Lack of social connection may pose as much of a risk as smoking, drinking too much, or leading a sedentary lifestyle. Friends are even tied to longevity. One Swedish study found that, along with physical activity, maintaining a rich network of friends can add significant years to your life. But close friendships don't just happen. Many of us struggle to meet people and develop quality connections. Whatever your age or circumstances, though, it's never too late to make new friends, reconnect with old ones, and greatly improve your social life, emotional health, and overall well-being.

While society often idealizes romantic relationships as the key to happiness, research shows that friendships are even more vital to our well-being. True friends bring joy, reduce stress, and help prevent loneliness.

Strong social connections aren't just good for the mind—they benefit the body too.

Let me share some stories on friendship.......

Society's Focus on Romance: Ananya always believed that finding "the one" would complete her life. She jumped from one relationship to another, thinking love would bring her lasting happiness. But even when she was in a relationship, she felt something was missing. It wasn't until a spontaneous road trip with her childhood best friend that she felt truly joyful—laughing, being herself, and feeling understood. She realized friendship gave her something romance couldn't.

Society may glorify romance, but true happiness often comes from deep friendships.

Friends Boost Mental Health: After moving to a new city, Ramesh felt overwhelmed, stressed, and alone. He didn't know anyone, and work pressures kept piling up. One day, he joined a weekend photography club. Slowly, he built friendships there. Talking to them, sharing meals, and simply laughing lifted his spirits. His anxiety decreased, and he found joy in small things again.

Good friends relieve stress, prevent loneliness, and boost happiness.

Friendships and Physical Health: Eighty-year-old Mrs. Fernandes never missed her morning walk—not just for exercise, but to meet her walking group. They shared stories, checked on each other, and laughed together. Despite her age, she remained active and cheerful. Doctors were amazed at her health and energy.

Strong friendships can help you live longer and stay healthier—just like exercise.

Friendships Take Effort: Vikram often complained about feeling alone but rarely reached out to old friends. One day, he took a chance and messaged an old college buddy. They met for coffee, and soon, started meeting regularly. That one message rekindled a friendship that brought joy and support into his life.

Friendships don't just happen—you have to reach out, nurture them, and stay open.

Making good friends—and keeping those friendships strong—is one of the most valuable things you can do for your well-being and happiness. Here's a simple, honest guide to help you do both:

How to Make Good Friends

1. **Be Yourself**
   Don't try to impress or pretend. Real friendships are built on authenticity.
   Share your true interests, thoughts, and values.

2. **Show Up**
   Join clubs, events, volunteering groups, or classes where people gather regularly.

Attend social functions, even if you feel shy at first. Familiarity breeds connection.

3. **Start Small**

   A smile, eye contact, and a "hi" can go a long way.

   Ask open-ended questions like "What do you think about this place?" or "What are you into?"

4. **Be Curious and Listen**

   Good friends are good listeners.

   Show genuine interest. People naturally like those who care about them.

5. **Be Kind and Helpful**

   Small acts of kindness—remembering birthdays, offering help—show you care.

   Be trustworthy and dependable.

How to Keep Good Friendships

1. **Nurture the Bond**

   Stay in touch. A short message, call, or meme sent regularly can make a big difference.

   Don't wait for them to reach out—take initiative too.

2. **Be There—Emotionally**

   Celebrate their wins, support them in their struggles.

   A good friend listens without judgment and comforts without trying to fix everything.

3. **Respect Boundaries**

   Understand your friend's needs, space, and preferences.

   Don't take it personally if they need time alone.

4. **Resolve Conflicts Gently**
   Disagreements happen. Talk things out with honesty and care. Apologize when you're wrong and forgive when you can.

5. **Grow Together**
   Encourage each other's goals, dreams, and growth.
   Accept change. True friendship allows people to evolve while staying connected.
   Let me give you a Bonus Tip

Don't rush—deep friendships take time.

Value quality over quantity—one good friend is worth more than ten shallow ones.

Give what you seek—if you want loyalty be loyal; if you want empathy be empathetic.

When Maya moved to a new city for work, she found herself surrounded by strangers. Every day after work, she would sit on the same park bench, watching people pass by, too shy to start a conversation.

One evening, an older woman named Asha sat beside her. She smiled, offered a piece of chocolate, and said, "This bench is magical. You sit here enough, you make a friend."

Maya chuckled but took the chocolate. They talked a little that day, and more the next. Eventually, they began meeting regularly—sometimes in silence, sometimes sharing stories, sometimes just watching the sky change colors.

Years passed, and Maya made other friends, but Asha remained her closest. Not because they did exciting things together, but because they *showed up*, listened, and quietly grew roots into each other's lives.

Friendship, Maya learned, didn't always begin with fireworks. Sometimes, it begins with a smile and a bench.

"Friendship isn't about who you've known the longest. It's about who walks into your life, says 'I'm here for you,' and proves it."

As we journey through life, we inevitably come to realize that many aspects of our existence lie beyond our control. We do not have the power to choose our parents or our genetic makeup, nor can we influence the unpredictable events that unfold in the world around us. However, amidst these uncontrollable factors, there remains one crucial area where we do hold agency—the people we allow into our inner circle, particularly our friends.

Unlike family or fate, friendship is a conscious choice. The friends we choose can significantly shape the quality of our lives. The right friendships can bring joy, support, and depth to our experiences, enriching our lives in meaningful and lasting ways. On the other hand, poor choices in friendships can lead to stress, disappointment, and emotional turmoil.

Recognizing the importance of this choice, it becomes essential to reflect on the kind of people we surround ourselves with. Choosing friends who uplift, inspire, and share values that align with our own can transform our lives for the better. These are the friendships that bring beauty and balance, especially when life feels uncertain or challenging.

We should remember however, that everything centers on the thoughtful and intentional selection of friends—those who add richness to our journey, bring positivity to our days, and help us grow into our best selves.

CHAPTER SIX

Open Communication

Do you know that open communication serves as the glue that holds the H-T-R-O formula together !!!!!

Source: Adobe Stock

They say silence can be golden—but in relationships, silence can also be dangerous.

A missed conversation today can become tomorrow's misunderstanding. A truth left unspoken can quietly grow into distance, resentment, or mistrust. Open communication is the antidote—it's the invisible thread that keeps connections strong, honest, and alive.

It's more than just speaking; it's about creating a safe space where honesty, empathy, and understanding can flow freely.

It involves:

- **Active Listening** – Being fully present, absorbing not just words but emotions, and responding with genuine interest.
- **Clear and Honest Expression** – Speaking truthfully and directly, without the shadow of fear or assumption.
- **Empathy and Understanding** – Stepping into someone else's shoes, validating their perspective, and making them feel seen.
- **Feedback and Dialogue** – Encouraging conversations that go both ways, where questions and ideas are welcomed.
- **Respectful Communication** – Holding onto respect, even when opinions clash.

The rewards are immense: deeper trust, stronger teams, fewer misunderstandings, and solutions born from collaboration instead of conflict.

Below are real-life-inspired moments that capture the beauty and impact of open communication in action.

1. The Office Misunderstanding

Ravi was drowning in work, but never said a word. His manager, Meena, thought everything was fine—after all, Ravi never complained. One day, stress boiled over, and Ravi's frustration spilled out in a team meeting. Surprised, Meena invited him for a private chat. That conversation revealed months of silent burnout. Meena listened, adjusted his workload, and introduced regular check-ins. The tension lifted—not just for Ravi, but for the whole team.

💡*When we speak up, we break the cycle of silent suffering.*

2. Between Friends

Sana and Priya had been inseparable since school. But lately, Priya felt like she was fading into the background as Sana's new job consumed her time. Instead of letting the distance grow, Priya gently told Sana how she felt. Sana's face softened—she had no idea. They agreed to schedule monthly meet-ups, no matter how busy life got.

💡*Kind honesty keeps friendships alive.*

3. The Parent Trap

Aryan, 13, was glued to his phone. His mother, frustrated, assumed he was wasting hours scrolling aimlessly. One evening, she confronted him sharply. Tears welled in his eyes as he revealed he was being bullied and had been finding comfort in online chats. Her anger melted into regret. She promised to listen without judgment from then on. Their relationship shifted from distant to deeply connected.

💡*Listening before judging can transform a bond.*

4. The Community Garden

In a small neighborhood garden, older residents wanted to fill the space with colorful flowers, while younger volunteers preferred growing vegetables. Tensions brewed until they finally sat down to talk. Flowers meant beauty and nostalgia; vegetables meant practicality and self-sufficiency. After hearing each other out, they decided to split the plot—half blooms, half produce. The garden thrived, and so did their sense of unity.

When voices are heard, solutions bloom.

5. The Classroom Silence

Riya was the quietest student in Mr. Thomas's class. He assumed she wasn't interested in participating—until one writing assignment revealed the truth. In a heartfelt essay, Riya confessed her fear of public speaking and her wish for help. Mr. Thomas took it to heart, giving her small, safe opportunities to speak. Slowly, Riya's voice grew stronger.

Communication doesn't always come as spoken words—sometimes, it's written from the heart.

Open communication isn't just a skill—it's a daily choice. It's the bridge between misunderstanding and connection, between frustration and collaboration. And often, it's the quiet, courageous act of saying, *"This is how I feel"* that changes everything.

Sometimes, writing can also be a form of open communication—and a powerful one.

Please Attempt The Below Open Communication Quiz

Multiple Choice Questions

Choose the best answer.

1. What is the main goal of open communication?
   a) To dominate the conversation
   b) To express anger freely
   c) To promote understanding and trust
   d) To agree with everyone

2. Which of the following is a key element of open communication?
   a) Interrupting to make your point
   b) Avoiding eye contact
   c) Active listening
   d) Talking more than others

3. What does active listening involve?
   a) Waiting for your turn to speak
   b) Repeating everything the speaker says
   c) Giving full attention, understanding, and responding appropriately
   d) Judging the speaker silently

4. Which of the following hinders open communication?
   a) Empathy
   b) Blame
   c) Clarifying questions
   d) Non-verbal cues

5. Open communication is most effective when…
   a) Only the leader speaks
   b) Everyone feels safe to share honestly
   c) All conversations are formal
   d) Emotions are kept out of it

True or False

6. Open communication requires both speaking honestly and listening respectfully.
   True / False
7. It is okay to assume what someone means in open communication.
   True / False
8. Giving feedback in open communication means focusing only on what went wrong.
   True / False
9. Asking clarifying questions is a good way to support open communication.
   True / False
10. In open communication, non-verbal cues such as body language and tone of voice are important.
    True / False

Short Answer / Reflective Questions

11. What does open communication mean to you in your own words?

12. Share an example of a time you practiced open communication. What was the outcome?
13. Why do you think trust is important in open communication?
14. What are two things you can do to become a better communicator?
15. How can open communication help in resolving conflicts?

Why H-T-R-O Matters in Open Communication

When I first joined a new project last year, I walked into the conference room with a mix of excitement and nerves. It was my dream assignment, but I quickly noticed something strange. People spoke in half-sentences, avoided eye contact, and rarely disagreed — at least, not out loud. On the surface, everything seemed fine. But beneath it, tension hummed like a silent current.

It wasn't until a small misunderstanding exploded into a major conflict that I realized the truth: the four pillars of healthy communication — Honesty, Trust, Respect, and Open Communication — were missing.

Honesty — Speaking the Uncomfortable Truth

One of my teammates, Meera, admitted later that she had spotted a mistake in our design weeks earlier but didn't speak up. "I didn't want to hurt anyone's feelings," she said quietly.

The problem? That silence cost us time, money, and a little bit of faith in one another.

Honesty doesn't mean being blunt or cruel. It means saying what you mean without hiding behind half-truths, owning mistakes, and being transparent — even when it feels uncomfortable. Without it, trust erodes.

Trust — The Bridge That Carries Vulnerability

Trust in our team was fragile. People kept their guard up, afraid that speaking openly might be used against them.

It took months of consistent follow-through — meeting deadlines, keeping promises, admitting when we didn't know something — for trust to return. Slowly, we began to share ideas more freely, knowing the other person wouldn't mock or betray us.

Trust isn't built overnight, but it can be broken in seconds. It's the bridge that lets people meet halfway without fear.

Respect — Valuing the Person Behind the Opinion

One turning point came when Arjun and Priya disagreed passionately on a design choice. Instead of rolling his eyes or shutting her down, Arjun leaned forward and said, "I see where you're coming from — can you walk me through your thinking?"

That moment shifted the tone of our meetings. Respect doesn't mean you always agree — it means you treat people's ideas and feelings as worthy of space. You listen, avoid judgment, and accept differences without trying to erase them.

Open Communication — The Oxygen That Keeps Teams Alive

When we finally embraced open communication, meetings felt different.

We started asking open-ended questions, listening without planning our rebuttals, and validating each other's feelings. Disagreements became discussions, not battles.

We learned to:

- Listen actively — giving our full attention instead of glancing at our phones.
- Speak with kindness and honesty — using "I" statements instead of accusations.
- Follow up — showing we remembered and cared about what someone shared.

Bit by bit, our team transformed from a group of cautious colleagues into a genuine unit that respected, trusted, and supported each other.

Addressing problems early became our golden rule. We didn't let misunderstandings sit in the dark where they could grow into resentment. We spoke up, we listened, and we fixed things together.

The result was not just a successful project, but bonds that lasted far beyond it.

Whether it's in a marriage, a friendship, or a workplace, H–T–R–O is the difference between just getting along and truly connecting.

Without honesty, trust, respect, and open communication, relationships survive at best — but with them, they *thrive*.

Effective communication goes beyond just exchanging information. It involves genuinely connecting with others — making them feel seen, heard, and valued. Strong communication builds trust, deepens relationships, and promotes understanding. Here are essential techniques to foster authentic connection through communication:

1. Active Listening

Focus fully on the speaker — avoid interrupting or formulating your response while they talk.

Use **non-verbal cues** like nodding or maintaining eye contact to show you're engaged.

Reflect back what you hear (e.g., "So you're saying…" or "It sounds like…").

2. Use Open-Ended Questions

Encourage deeper sharing by avoiding yes/no questions.

Examples:

"How did that make you feel?"

"What was the most important part of that experience?"

This invites the other person to open up and feel heard.

3. Practice Empathy

Try to **feel with**, not just understand.

Show compassion by acknowledging emotions:

"That must have been really hard for you."

"I can see why you'd feel that way."

Empathy bridges the emotional gap between people.

4. Be Present

Put away distractions (like your phone).

Give undivided attention — this shows respect and care.

Mind your tone, body language, and facial expressions.

Connection fades when attention is divided.

5. Speak with Honesty and Kindness

Be clear and authentic in what you say.

Avoid blaming or criticizing. Use "I" statements instead of "you" statements.

"I felt hurt when that happened." (Instead of: "You always ignore me.")

Honest communication strengthens trust.

6. Validate the Other Person's Experience

You don't need to agree to validate.

Say things like:

"I hear you."

"It makes sense you'd feel that way."

Validation makes people feel seen and accepted.

7. Match Energy and Tone Appropriately

Mirror body language or tone (without mimicking) to build rapport.

Be calm and respectful, especially in difficult conversations.

This creates harmony and understanding.

8. Know When to Pause

Silence can be powerful.

Allow time for processing emotions or thoughts.

Don't rush to fill every gap.

Sometimes connection happens in the quiet spaces.

9. Offer Encouragement and Appreciation

Small affirmations build connection:

"I appreciate you sharing that."

"Thanks for being honest with me."

Gratitude nurtures emotional safety.

10. Follow Up and Show Care

Remember what people share with you — ask about it later.

"How did that meeting go?" or "You mentioned your mom was sick, how is she now?"

Caring follow-ups show that the connection continues beyond the moment.

Connections happen when communication is rooted in presence, empathy, and respect. These techniques not only make conversations meaningful but also create a space where people feel safe to be themselves.

Addressing problems early is a key strategy for maintaining healthy relationships, productive workplaces, and personal well-being. When issues are ignored or minimized, they often grow in complexity and intensity, leading to misunderstandings, resentment, and long-term damage.

Why It Matters

Prevents Miscommunication: Small misunderstandings can quickly snowball if not clarified in time.

Preserves Relationships: Timely dialogue shows respect and care, preventing emotional distance.

Reduces Stress: Avoiding conflict may seem easier in the moment, but unresolved issues often create ongoing tension.

Fosters Growth: Addressing problems early can lead to better understanding, personal development, and improved systems.

Steps to Address Issues Early

1. **Recognize the Problem:** Be honest with yourself about what's bothering you.
2. **Choose the Right Time:** Don't confront in the heat of the moment. Choose a calm setting.
3. **Communicate Clearly:** Use "I" statements to express your experience without blame.
4. **Listen Actively:** Let the other person share their side without interruption.
5. **Seek Resolution Together:** Focus on solutions, not winning the argument.
6. **Follow Up:** Ensure the resolution is working and continue to build trust.

And Finally:

Don't wait too long — address things when they're still small.

Stay respectful and calm, even if emotions run high.

Practice empathy — try to see things from the other person's perspective.

Here are some case studies and examples centered on the values of Honesty, Trust, Respect, and Open Communication (HTRO). These stories come from various settings—workplace, personal relationships, schools, and communities—to show how these principles can either strengthen or break down relationships depending on how they're applied.

1. Workplace – Rebuilding Trust After a Mistake

Case Study: The Marketing Mishap

Scenario:

In a marketing agency, a team member mistakenly sent a draft campaign to a high-profile client without approval. The client was upset, and the team was under pressure.

Action Taken:

The employee owned up immediately, explaining the mistake honestly to both the team leader and the client. The manager supported the employee, communicated openly with the client, and took responsibility as a team. They worked together to fix the issue.

Outcome:

The client appreciated the transparency and stayed with the agency. The employee wasn't punished but instead was trained further. Trust within the team grew because of the respectful handling of the error.

Lesson:

Honesty and open communication can turn a potentially destructive situation into an opportunity to build deeper trust.

2. Family – Teen Confides in Parent

Example: Breaking the Silence

Scenario:

A teenage daughter started coming home late and seemed withdrawn. Her parents were concerned but chose not to confront her harshly.

Action Taken:

One evening, her mother gently said, "I've noticed you've been quiet lately. I want you to know you can talk to me about anything." This opened the door for the teen to share that she was being bullied and felt ashamed.

Outcome:

The open, respectful communication allowed them to seek help together. It deepened their bond and built lasting trust.

Lesson:

Respecting someone's emotional space while being open and honest can help build bridges of trust in families.

3. School – Classroom Conflict Resolution

Case Study: Student Cheating Incident

Scenario:

A student was caught cheating on a test. The teacher called the student for a private conversation.

Action Taken:

Instead of punishing outright, the teacher said, "I value honesty and want to understand what led to this." The students admitted they were overwhelmed and afraid to fail.

Outcome:

The student was given a second chance with a study plan. Over time, the student began to approach the teacher for help, showing improved performance and character.

Lesson:

Respect and openness in addressing difficult situations can create an environment of growth rather than shame.

4. Community – Neighbor Dispute

Example: Noise Complaint Turned Cooperation

Scenario:

Two neighbors were at odds due to one hosting loud late-night gatherings.

Action Taken:

Instead of filing a formal complaint, the affected neighbor knocked and politely expressed how the noise was affecting their sleep. The host listened without defensiveness and apologized sincerely.

Outcome:

They agreed on quiet hours and even began sharing meals during the day. Their relationship changed from tension to trust.

Lesson:

Respectful, honest dialogue often leads to unexpected connections and cooperation.

5. Corporate Leadership – CEO Transparency During Crisis

Case Study: Financial Downturn

Scenario:

During a downturn, a tech startup faced potential layoffs. The CEO could have kept quiet until the last moment, but chose otherwise.

Action Taken:

In a company-wide meeting, she laid out the financials, explained the challenges, and asked for input. She promised to avoid layoffs and took a pay cut herself. Employees volunteered creative cost-cutting ideas.

Outcome:

They weathered the crisis together. Morale improved. Employees felt respected and trusted—and gave it back.

Lesson:

Honest and open communication at leadership levels inspires trust, loyalty, and collaborative solutions.

Let's reflect on all the case studies and answer these questions

1. Which of these cases most resonated with you, and why?
2. How do you usually respond to mistakes—your own or others'?
3. Have you ever experienced the power of open communication in resolving a conflict?
4. What role does respect play when delivering honest feedback?
5. In what areas of your life can you practice more trust and transparency?

The magic of the H–T–R–O formula lies in its harmony. When Honesty, Trust, Respect, and Open Communication are present and nurtured, they don't just coexist; they amplify each other. Together, they form a resilient bond, a shelter strong enough to weather life's storms. In this space, partners feel secure, valued, and deeply understood.

As I close this book, my hope is that you carry with you not just words, but a renewed vision of what's possible in your relationships. We've explored what it truly means to connect—to share life with honesty, to build trust that can withstand trials, to offer respect that honors differences, and to communicate openly from the heart. These are not lofty ideals to admire from afar; they are the foundation stones of lasting, meaningful connection.

H–T–R–O is not a quick fix, nor a single grand gesture. It's a daily choice—a rhythm you return to again and again. Relationships that embody these principles still face misunderstandings, hardships, and moments of uncertainty. But what sets them apart is the shared commitment to work through those moments together, emerging stronger each time.

This journey begins within. Honesty starts in quiet moments when you listen to your own heart and speak your truth, even when it's hard. Trust grows not only when others keep their promises, but when you show yourself that you can rise after every fall. Respect begins in the way you speak to yourself in your thoughts, how you honor your worth, and how you refuse to diminish yourself to fit into someone else's comfort. And open communication isn't only about speaking your truth to others—it's also about listening to your inner voice and asking, What do I need? What do I feel? What do I want to create?

Now, imagine a world where these values aren't rare treasures, but everyday practice. Picture couples whose love is unshaken because it's anchored in honesty. Picture friendships where trust runs so deep that vulnerability feels safe. Picture families where respect makes every voice matter, and open communication flows as naturally as breathing. This is a world where relationships don't just survive—they flourish.

This isn't a dream. It begins with you.

One relationship at a time.

One conversation at a time.

One choice at a time.

Let H–T–R–O be your compass when the path is unclear, your anchor when the winds are strong, and your reminder that the best love—whether for yourself or for another—is love that nurtures growth, offers safety, and welcomes authenticity.

Because love rooted in honesty, trust, respect, and open communication is more than a feeling—it's a living partnership. It's a connection that stands the test of time, a safe haven where both hearts can grow without fear.

May your relationships—starting with the one you have with yourself—be grounded in these four principles. May they give you strength in storms, joy in stillness, and a lifetime of moments worth cherishing. In the end, the greatest gift you can offer—to yourself and to those you love—is to live the H–T–R–O way:

Be honest. Build trust. Show respect. Keep the conversation open.

Do this, and your relationships will not merely endure—they will become sanctuaries of strength, joy, and belonging. And it all begins, right here, with you.

CHAPTER SEVEN

Conclusion

As I close this book, my hope is that you walk away with a renewed sense of purpose and a deeper belief in the power of authentic connection.

Throughout these pages, we've journeyed through the heart of what it means to truly relate to another human being—not just to coexist, but to connect. We've reflected on the essential pillars that hold every meaningful relationship together: honesty, trust, respect, and open communication. These are not lofty ideals meant only for perfect moments; they are the quiet, daily choices that transform ordinary connections into extraordinary ones.

These four principles—H-T-R-O—are not magic formulas. They do not erase conflict or prevent life's inevitable storms. But they *do* give us the strength to stand together through them. Relationships rooted in these values don't avoid difficulty—they transcend it. What makes such relationships last isn't the absence of pain, but the presence of unwavering commitment and shared values that deepen with time.

More than anything, this journey is a commitment to *yourself.*

To practice honesty is to embrace your truth—even when it's uncomfortable.

To build trust is to be consistent and kind, not just with others, but also with yourself.

To show respect is to honor differences, value boundaries, and treat every soul with dignity—including your own.

To communicate openly is to let your heart be seen, and to listen with the intent to understand.

These are not always easy paths. They call for courage, vulnerability, and grace. But in return, they offer the most precious gift of all: real, lasting connection.

As you step into the next chapter of your life, may you carry these principles not only into your relationships with others, but into the relationship you hold with yourself.

Be honest about your needs.

Trust your inner strength.

Respect your worth.

Speak gently and truthfully to your own heart.

Imagine, for a moment, a world where these values are lived out by more people—where partners speak with honesty, where friends uplift with trust, where families honor each other with respect, and where every conversation becomes a chance for deeper connection. That world is not far away. It starts with you.

With each relationship you nurture. With each moment, you choose H-T-R-O.

So, as you turn the final page, don't leave these words behind. Let them guide you. Let them steady you. Let them inspire you to love and live with purpose.

Because a life built on honesty, trust, respect, and open communication isn't just a life well-lived—it's a life deeply connected, richly meaningful, and profoundly whole.

In a world saturated with noise, opinions, distractions, and half-truths, it's easy to forget the foundational principle that holds human relationships together: honesty. Whether in friendships, romantic relationships, families, or workplaces, honesty is not just a moral virtue — it is the bedrock of genuine connection.

We live in an era where curated lives dominate social media, public figures carefully sculpt their images, and people often wear masks just to "fit in." In such a climate, honesty can seem outdated or even risky. And yet, deep down, every human being longs for connection — not just surface-level interaction, but authentic, soul-deep connection. That kind of connection is impossible without honesty.

Honesty creates the conditions for trust, and trust is the soil where all meaningful relationships grow. When we are honest, we show up as our true selves. We allow others to know us, and we create space for them to be known. Without honesty, we may interact, but we will never connect.

When honesty becomes the norm, it brings about a radical transformation in the quality of our interactions.

Honesty clears away the fog of assumptions, misunderstandings, and silent resentment. Instead of guessing what the other person feels or needs, you know — because they told you. Likewise, others don't have to decipher your hints or decode your silences.

Clarity leads to fewer conflicts and more effective problem-solving. Even when disagreements arise, honest communication helps people stay on the same team.

We don't connect through perfection — we connect through truth. Sharing your joys, doubts, struggles, and dreams honestly creates emotional intimacy. It invites others into your inner world and gives them permission to do the same.

This is especially powerful in friendships and romantic relationships. Emotional honesty — such as "I'm afraid of losing you," or "I feel distant lately" — can be the bridge that reconnects two people drifting apart.

Living honestly is not just a gift to others; it's a gift to yourself. When you are truthful about who you are, what you want, and what you feel, you experience a kind of **freedom**. You stop living in fear of being found out. You stop exhausting yourself by pretending. You live in alignment — a life where your values, words, and actions are in harmony.

On the flip side, dishonesty — whether in the form of outright lies, half-truths, or emotional withholding — erodes connection at its core.

If honesty is so foundational, why do we so often shy away from it? But while honesty is sometimes painful in the short-term, dishonesty always leads to more pain in the long-term. Becoming a more honest person is a daily choice — and a courageous one.

At its core, honesty is not just about accuracy — it's about **love**. It says, "I respect you enough to tell you the truth." It's an act of bravery, humility, and integrity. And while it may feel risky, it is the **only path to real connection**.

In a world of illusion and facades, honesty is a breath of fresh air. It is the doorway through which all meaningful relationships must pass. If you want relationships that are not only deep but durable — friendships that last, marriages that thrive, teams that work, families that stay close — build them on the bedrock of honesty.

Trust is not a one-time act or a simple transaction—it is the silent thread that weaves through every meaningful connection in our lives. It forms the foundation of our relationships, the structure of our communities, and the soul of our character. In writing this book, one truth has emerged more clearly than anything else: **trust is both a gift and a responsibility.**

To trust is to be vulnerable, to open ourselves up to the possibility of being hurt—but also to the deeper possibility of being deeply known and valued. To be trustworthy is to commit, again and again, to honesty, integrity, and empathy, even when it is inconvenient or uncomfortable.

We live in a world that often rewards speed, surface-level impressions, and short-term gain. But trust is built slowly, in moments both big and small—through consistency, kindness, transparency, and follow-through. It is easily damaged and painstakingly repaired, but its worth is immeasurable.

Whether in personal relationships, professional environments, or our relationship with ourselves, trust gives us the courage to be human. It helps us heal, grow, and collaborate. It transforms transactional interactions into meaningful bonds and fear-based silence into open communication.

As I close this book, consider this: How are you building trust in your life today? Who trusts you—and why? And how can you deepen that trust, protect it, and extend it to others who need it most?

Trust is not a finish line. It is a daily choice—a quiet revolution we commit to in our hearts and actions.

And in the end, perhaps the greatest legacy we can leave behind is this: *I was someone who could be trusted.*

Respect is more than just politeness or good manners — it is the foundation of every meaningful human interaction. Whether in personal relationships, professional environments, or everyday encounters with strangers, respect is what allows us to coexist with dignity and harmony.

When we respect others, we acknowledge their worth, listen to their voices, and treat their perspectives with consideration. Likewise, self-respect empowers us to set healthy boundaries, make wise choices, and live with confidence and integrity.

In a world that often highlights differences and division, respect becomes a bridge — one that connects hearts, builds trust, and fosters understanding. It does not require agreement, only the willingness to see humanity in others.

As we conclude this reflection on respect, let us remember:

- Respect must begin within — by valuing ourselves.
- It must be extended outward — through our words, actions, and choices.
- And it must be practiced consistently — especially when it is difficult.

In showing respect, we do not diminish ourselves; we elevate everyone. And in doing so, we create spaces — in homes, schools, workplaces, and communities — where people can truly flourish.

Let respect be not just a virtue we talk about, but a way of life we commit to living every day.

Open communication is the heartbeat of every healthy relationship—whether personal, professional, or social. It creates space for honesty, builds trust, nurtures respect, and allows people to connect with each other on a deeper, more meaningful level. When we communicate openly, we not only express ourselves more clearly, but we also show others that their thoughts, feelings, and perspectives matter.

Throughout life, miscommunication, assumptions, and silence can create distance and even damage relationships. But choosing to speak truthfully, listen actively, and engage with empathy can bridge gaps and resolve misunderstandings before they grow. Open communication empowers us to handle conflict constructively, celebrate differences, and work together toward shared goals.

It's not always easy—being vulnerable requires courage, and listening with patience demands maturity. But the rewards are profound: healthier relationships, deeper understanding, and a stronger sense of connection.

As you move forward, remember that open communication isn't just about talking—it's about creating a safe space where voices are heard, feelings are validated, and mutual growth becomes possible. Practice it consistently, and you'll discover its transformative power in every area of your life.

Let your words be a bridge, not a barrier.

Take a moment to reflect and fill in your responses to each question in the checklist under the respective categories. Invite your partner to do the same—honestly and neutrally. Together, this exercise becomes a powerful mirror for your relationship, helping you both gain clarity, understanding, and alignment.

Once you've completed the checklist and reviewed your answers, you may realize the wisdom you were searching for was within you all along. Who knows—you might just save yourself a trip to the astrologer or pandit… and spare your wallet their hefty consultation fees. 😉✨

Category	Checklist Item	Your Input (Neutral)	Your Partner's Input (Neutral)	Final Decision/ Note	Fill Rate (On Agreed Points)
LIFE PURPOSE & PERSONAL IDENTITY	What is my core life purpose?				
	What do I want to be remembered for?				
	What is my vision for the next 5/10/20 years?				
	What is my personal mission statement?				
	What are my non-negotiable values?				
CORE BELIEFS, LIKES & DISLIKES	My spiritual/ religious beliefs				
	My political and social views				
	My personal likes (hobbies, nature, reading, music, etc.)				
	My dislikes (crowded places, loud behavior, negative people, etc.)				
	Pet peeves and triggers				

FLEXIBILITY vs NON-FLEXIBILITY	**Open to relocating?**				
	Open to career changes or business shifts?				
	Open to different parenting styles or choices?				
	Flexible with diet/lifestyle differences?				
	Rigid about any cultural, moral, or ethical views?				
PHYSICAL & MENTAL HEALTH FINANCIAL STATUS & GOALS	**Current health conditions (if any)**				
	Diet plan or restrictions				
	Exercise routines				
	Sleep pattern and needs				
	Stress triggers and coping mechanisms				
	Any medication or supplements				
	Need for health insurance plans?				
	Monthly income & expenses				

	Savings & investments				
	Ongoing debts/ loans (amount, purpose, timeline)				
	Emergency fund setup?				
	Retirement plans or insurance?				
	Short-term (1–2 years) goals				
	Medium-term (3–5 years) goals				
	Long-term (10+ years) dreams				
	Shared financial goals				
RELATIONSHIP EXPECTATIONS	**Quality time preferences**				
	Communication style				
	Conflict resolution style				
	Sexual intimacy expectations				
	Social life & friendships management				
	Individual space & freedom understanding				

FAMILY PLANS	**Views on having children**				
	Parenting style & values				
	Relationship with in-laws				
	Family planning or fertility discussions				
LIFESTYLE & PREFERENCES	**Favorite colors**				
	Favorite cuisines and food habits				
	Preferred dress style				
	Travel style				
	Preferred cities/ countries to live				
	Dream house vision				
LEARNING & PERSONAL GROWTH	**Favorite books/ authors**				
	Preferred topics of learning				
	Passion projects or hobbies				
	Willingness to grow together through coaching?				

DAILY & WEEKLY ROUTINES	**Wake-up & bedtime preference**				
	Ideal morning routine				
	Weekend habits				
	Me-time requirements				
	Digital & phone usage habits				
COMMUNICATION & EMOTIONAL NEEDS LIFE LEGACY & EXIT PLAN	**How do I express emotions?**				
	How do I like to be supported during tough times?				
	Boundaries I expect				
	Apology & forgiveness style				
	Love language				
	Will & asset planning				
	World contribution goals				
	Retirement life vision				
	Final wishes or funeral preferences				

COUPLE ALIGNMENT & GOALS	**What does a successful marriage mean to us?**				
	Top 3 shared dreams				
	3 red flags or fears to discuss				
	Staying connected and growing plan				
	What if we grow differently?				
MUTUAL DECISIONS	**Wedding plans & rituals**				
	Where to live post-marriage?				
	Joint bank accounts or separation?				
	Career growth and support				
	Holiday and celebration plans				
	Couple rituals				
NOTE: Explanations On Fill Rate: If Both Parties Agree, Then It Will Be Considered As Point One On Each Parameter, And If Either Of The Parties Disagrees On Any Parameter, Then The Fill Rate Point Will Be Zero.					

As I bring *Beyond Physical Romance* to a close, I return to the simplest truth — meaningful relationships are not sustained by intensity alone, but by intimacy, intention, and integrity. They are not built in a day, nor do they fall apart overnight. Like a garden, they flourish only with consistent attention, gentle care, thoughtful pruning, and the right nourishment. In the garden of lasting love, the richest nutrients are Honesty, Trust, Respect, and Open Communication.

When Aarav first met Meera, the connection was instant — late-night talks, stolen glances, and a warmth that made them believe this was love in its purest form. But as months passed, they began to see that attraction alone wasn't enough to sustain a relationship.

The turning point came during a harsh winter. Meera fell ill, bedridden for weeks. The candlelit dinners and long drives were replaced by Aarav making soup at midnight, wrapping her in blankets, and reading aloud to her until she fell asleep. There was no glamour, no stage — just quiet care.

Months later, Aarav's career hit rock bottom. Self-doubt crept in, but Meera never wavered. She listened without interrupting, reminded him of his strengths, and celebrated even the smallest victories.

It dawned on them: *love is not tested in moments of passion, but in seasons of struggle.* True romance grows when you protect each other's vulnerabilities and nurture each other's dreams.

This principle also lived in Aarav's role as a leader. In his company, he learned that a team's loyalty wasn't built by grand speeches, but by being present during failures, protecting his people in crises, and celebrating their growth. Just like in his marriage, leadership meant standing by someone's side even when it's uncomfortable, uncertain, or inconvenient.

They realized their bond had moved beyond a physical romance — into a deeper love built on trust, respect, and shared resilience. And in both love and leadership, those are the ties that truly last.

Whether in love or leadership, the truest measure of a relationship is not how it thrives in easy seasons, but how it endures in storms. Physical attraction may spark the beginning, but it is trust, respect, and unwavering support that write the lasting chapters. When you choose to stand beside someone in their weakest moments, you are telling them, *"You are not alone, and I believe in you."* That is where hearts are won, teams are built, and legacies are formed — beyond physical romance.

If there's one takeaway you carry from this journey, let it be this: KISS — and no, not the lip-lock kind, but a mental and emotional embrace.

K For Keep it Kind — Kindness is the invisible thread that mends wounds, bridges differences, and keeps hearts warm even in the cold seasons of life. A soft word, a gentle touch, an unspoken understanding — they are often worth more than a thousand grand gestures.

I For Invite Intimacy — Not just the kind you see in movies, but the intimacy of truly being seen and heard. The late-night conversations, the quiet hand-holding in the middle of chaos, the trust that allows you to share your fears without fear of judgment.

S For Show up with Sincerity — Presence is a gift few truly give. When you're there, be there — heart, mind, and soul. Let your words mean what they say, and your silences carry understanding, not distance.

S For Stay Soulfully Connected — True connection doesn't fade when the lights dim or the years pass. It's in the way you still notice each other's smallest changes, the way you can sit in silence yet feel full, the way you grow not just alongside each other, but into each other's hearts.

In a world obsessed with spectacle — where love is often mistaken for grand drama and endless desire — remember this:

- It's the quiet power of kindness that steadies the storms.
- It's the courage to be emotionally naked that deepens the bond.
- It's the habit of honest presence that keeps the bridge between you strong.
- It's the choice to keep growing together that makes love last.

Love doesn't have to be loud to be real. Romance doesn't have to be physical to be fulfilling. Connection doesn't have to be perfect to be powerful.

So, keep it simple. Keep it soulful. Just KISS. And may your relationships always reach beyond the fleeting pull of the physical — into that rare, sacred space where two souls meet, lock eyes, and silently promise, *"I'm here, always."* A place where laughter feels like music, silences feel like poetry, and even storms outside the window only make you hold each other tighter because love like that doesn't just survive the weather — it dances in the rain.

And may your relationships always go *beyond* the physical.